The Feedback Fix

Praise for *The Feedback Fix*

"Shows the remarkable things that can happen when businesses, schools, and families rethink traditional feedback. Highly recommended." —**Marshall Goldsmith**, executive coach, business educator, and bestselling author of *Triggers*

"Most people dislike one thing more than giving feedback: receiving it. Joe Hirsch is here to fix that. This delightful, evidence-based book is a breath of fresh air, and I've already started trying out his terrific tips at work and at home." —**Adam Grant**, *New York Times* bestselling author of *Originals* and *Give and Take*

"The giving and receiving of feedback is fraught territory, easily the most challenging part of my work as a teacher. *The Feedback Fix* is a fantastic resource, with practical, actionable advice on how to formulate quality feedback for others and hear the constructive criticism and praise. I highly recommend this book and am grateful to Hirsch for writing so eloquently about a topic that makes me squirm with discomfort." —**Jessica Lahey**, *New York Times* bestselling author of *The Gift of Failure*

"Hirsch masterfully takes us on a journey that completely redefines what we think about learning, development, and performance. His book is smartly written, provocative, and insightful—a must-have for any curious learner or leader committed to unleashing potential around them." —**Rand Stagen**, Stagen Leadership Academy; former chairman, Conscious Capitalism, Inc.

"Finding mastery involves searching deep inside yourself, refining a craft, adjusting to feedback (both internally and externally), and authentically expressing oneself in a wide range of environments. *The Feedback Fix* drills into the value and mechanics of how to use feedback, how to give feedback, and how to accelerate growth." —**Michael Gervais**, PhD, high-performance psychology, Seattle Seahawks consultant

"Successful relationships are grounded in honesty, authenticity, and respectful communication. A cornerstone of effective parenting, marriages, teaching, and workplace success is the ability to give feedback on progress in a manner that promotes growth rather than resentment. Hirsch has written a fascinating and practical book that is presented in an engaging mix of studies, stories, and detailed explanations on how to transform feedback into an effective, energizing source of creativity, enhanced connection, and motivation for change. I know that the paradigm shift presented in this book will change the way I give feedback to my students, colleagues, and family members. I highly recommend this book for anybody who is seeking a novel perspective on this all-important aspect of effective relationships." —**David Pelcovitz**, PhD, Straus Chair in Psychology and Education, Azrieli Graduate School, Yeshiva University

"*The Feedback Fix* is relevant and timely across all disciplines and settings. Hirsch has gifted us with a roadmap for more productive, more courageous, and more authentic conversations that will lead to lasting and positive change." —**Michelle Kinder**, executive director, Momentous Institute

The Feedback Fix

Dump the Past, Embrace the Future, and Lead the Way to Change

JOE HIRSCH

ROWMAN & LITTLEFIELD
Lanham • Boulder • New York • London

Published by Rowman & Littlefield
A wholly owned subsidiary of The Rowman & Littlefield Publishing Group, Inc.
4501 Forbes Boulevard, Suite 200, Lanham, Maryland 20706
www.rowman.com

Unit A, Whitacre Mews, 26-34 Stannary Street, London SE11 4AB

British Library Cataloguing in Publication Information Available

Library of Congress Cataloging-in-Publication Data Available

ISBN 9781475826593 (cloth : alk. paper)
ISBN 9781475826616 (electronic)

∞™ The paper used in this publication meets the minimum requirements of
American National Standard for Information Sciences—Permanence of Paper
for Printed Library Materials, ANSI/NISO Z39.48-1992.

Printed in the United States of America

For Abby,
whose feedback changed everything.

Contents

Foreword

When I developed the concept of "feedforward" many years ago, I had no idea that it would have such a long life—or so many surprising applications.

In the beginning, I was simply looking for a better way to do performance appraisals. I had been an executive coach for several years when I observed that the employee reviews tended to be an uncomfortable, embarrassing, or downright painful experience, for both the giver and the receiver.

Successful leaders, who prided themselves on their drive and competence, had a particularly hard time hearing about their own failures and missteps. Often they came away determined to prove that the negative feedback was wrong. That approach was rarely helpful, either for the person or for the organization.

I designed feedforward as an alternative to traditional feedback. As Joe Hirsch notes in these pages, feedforward involves asking for advice about how to do better in the future. The listener collects the advice without judgment or comment, except to say thank you. He or she is free to discard anything irrelevant or unhelpful.

I found that successful executives were particularly eager to try it since it gave them a chance to accept a challenge without the burden of negative judgment. It empowered them to set a course for the future instead of dwelling on the past, which they couldn't change anyway. Inherently positive, it assumed their capacity to change. And it was faster and more efficient than traditional feedback. Many of them actually enjoyed the process, even describing it as fun! It became an important part of my coaching process.

I am delighted that feedforward has proved useful not just for me but also for many others. In this book, Joe Hirsch gives compelling examples of how individuals and organizations are using it, with remarkable results. If my books and articles haven't convinced you of the value of feedforward, *The Feedback Fix* surely will. Hirsch breaks down how it works and why it works, drawing on a trove of scientific research as well as his own reporting. From the halls of a mammoth multinational like Deloitte to a tiny school in Israel, and many places in between, he shows how feedforward is creating a quiet revolution in the way people work and live.

Particularly striking is how feedforward applies to educational settings. Instead of rating students on what they did in the past (the grading system familiar to most of us), Hirsch shows how some pioneering educators are asking their students positive and open-ended questions about how to solve problems in the future. In business, he shows how the principles of feedforward are helping individuals and teams look forward—and take the longest possible view of their own plans and potential. He also includes some poignant examples of how empowering feedforward can be for families.

This is a great point, and one I've tried to impress upon coaching clients and people at my seminars over the years. Feedforward is not just a tool for business success; it's also a life skill that can have dramatic consequences. For example, several years ago, I taught a one-day leadership course for a health-care organization in Oakland for about a thousand managers and union leaders. After my talk, a woman named Trudy Triner took the microphone to ask a question.

It turned out she didn't have a question, but rather a suggestion for me. She had attended many of my courses and read my books, she said. "You always talk about the value of asking direct reports, 'How can I be a better manager?' Or asking coworkers, 'How can I be a better team player?' Or asking customers, 'How can I be a better supplier?' And even asking partners or children, 'How can I be a better partner or better parent?'

"The one thing that you have left out that you should start teaching everyone is to ask their parents, 'How can I be a better daughter or a better son?'" It was true—I hadn't thought of that. But she had, and after my last course she had decided to call her mother, who lived in Arkansas at the end of a long country road.

Trudy went on to tell us how her mother had answered. It was pretty heartbreaking. "Now that Dad is dead, I live all alone," Trudy's mom said. "Every day I walk up that long drive to go to the mailbox. Almost every day there is nothing in the mailbox. This makes me feel very lonely. It would mean so much to me if you could just send me some cards, or pictures, or notes, so that when I walk to the mailbox, there will be a little something inside."

Trudy accepted the challenge and began sending cards, pictures, notes—and ticket stubs, flower seeds, tea bags, and pretty much anything that would fit into an envelope. She kept it up almost every day for two and a half years, until her mother died a week after being diagnosed with cancer. It cost Trudy nothing, and it meant everything to her mom, who in the last years of her life gained a more tangible connection to the daughter she loved.

That's just one example of how feedforward is simple to understand and do but profound in its consequences. This excellent book has many others. I am excited about what possibilities it will unlock for you.

Marshall Goldsmith
Executive coach, business educator, and New York Times–*bestselling author*
Ranked the number one leadership thinker in the world by Thinkers50

Acknowledgments

When I pick up a book, I always flip right to the acknowledgments. For me, it's like going backstage at a concert or behind the counter at a restaurant—you get to see how everything came together. Now, writing a book of my own, I am truly astonished and heartened by all the people who, in one way or another, made this project a reality. Writing is solitary work, but publishing is a team sport—and I feel blessed to have worked with such an amazing team. So, in no particular order, here are the individuals who thoughtfully carried *The Feedback Fix* across the goal line.

Marshall Goldsmith is in a class by himself. The world's leading business educator and executive coach, he has helped hundreds of top CEOs and their management teams address change in the workplace. I first learned about "feedforward" from Marshall, so it seems only right that his name appears on the cover, too. Thank you, Marshall.

The book you are reading exists because of the talented Sarah Jubar. She came to me out of nowhere with an unbelievable opportunity and made me believe that I could actually pull it off. If somewhere in these pages you come across an idea that stirs you, challenges you, or moves you to action, it's probably her doing. She's smart, professional, ridiculously thorough, and full of good ideas. In other words, she's my editor. Thank you, Sarah.

The team at Rowman & Littlefield made this project smooth from start to finish. Hats off to Tom Koerner, Carlie Wall, and the rest of the education department for their professionalism and assistance every step of the way. Dean Roxanis did a superb job handling the marketing effort. Patricia Stevenson ably pushed the project through production. Wanda Ditch gave the book its distinctive look. And Sally Rinehart designed the beautiful cover.

Thanks to Debbie Engel and Jennifer McGlucken for reading an early draft of the manuscript and for offering critical guidance about the business of books. Speaking of selling, I couldn't have done any of this without my street team of "fixers" who helped spread the word, break the mold, and offer guidance on everything from designing a website to producing a slick book trailer. You know who you are, and you are every bit a part of this story.

I am profoundly grateful to the people who enhanced this book by agreeing to let me share their stories: Ron Berger, Ashley Goodall, Elad Segev, Michael Gervais, Rand Stagen, Michelle Kinder, and Yolanda and Rudy Mendoza. In different ways, they are helping people discover a better version of themselves.

The best part about becoming an author is getting to meet and know other authors. For helping me overcome my rookie slump, deep appreciation goes out to Daniel Pink, Adam Grant, Jessica Lahey, Michael Bungay Sanier, and Neil Pasricha. You are among the classiest and most generous writers out there today.

A number of business leaders helped school this teacher on some of the leadership and management principles featured in these pages. They are Mike Preston at Deloitte, Ike Harris at Cisco, and Sunny Vanderbeck at Satori Capital. You are living examples of how big business can be big hearted. And to all the "Saturday seminars" I received from good friends over good food: Matthew Berke, Marc Blumberg, and Michael Rutner. Thanks for giving me a business education while standing on one foot.

So many people provided the right help at the right time, and I am indebted to Kat Adams, Monica Arellano, Karla Crow, April Hance, Kate Hawley, Hope Kahan, Jennifer Lauck, Alicia Lopez, Sarah McArthur, Katie Taylor, and Yitzhak Zuriel for coordinating calendars, opening doors, checking my facts, and responding to midnight requests for more information.

Even before I tried to write a book about feedback, I received a lot of it from family, mentors, and friends. My parents, Rosalyn and Irvin Hirsch, and in-laws, Marcie and Yaakov Calm, have steered me well when it counted the most. The professors at Yeshiva University's Azrieli Graduate School have kept me on track for much of my teaching career and doctoral training, which gave me a whole new understanding of data and research. And my colleagues and students at Akiba Academy—who by now feel more like family—have provided countless lessons in selflessness, passion, and persistence. From you, I learn more about myself every day.

Finally, to Ariel, Dov, Yakir, and Elisha, who have been giving me feedback since the day they were born, I share this book with you hoping that someday you'll get what you want by giving others what they need. And, of course, Abby—for the one who insists on leaving this part unspoken, the dedication says it all.

Introduction

A Butterfly Gets Its Wings

On a clear autumn morning in September, a six-year-old boy named Austin decided that he wanted to draw a butterfly. Not just any butterfly—a western tiger swallowtail. Swallowtails are large, colorful butterflies that can be spotted in urban parks and gardens across much of western North America, from the sun-dappled valleys of British Columbia down to the dusty plains of North Dakota. With its dramatic yellow-and-black striped body, forked hindwings, and blue-and-orange spots that run along its tail, the western tiger swallowtail is also one of the more complex-looking butterflies you might encounter out in the woodlands of Garden City, Idaho, a sleepy town of about eleven thousand that is home to lush gardens, an artist's district, and the Anser Charter School, where Austin had just begun first grade.

Students at Anser have developed a knack for creating high-quality work for authentic audiences. In what is now a school tradition, the kindergarten class completes a year-long study of birds and tops off the unit with a real-life project, creating detailed, hand-drawn cards that feature bird illustrations on one side and general information about them on the other. They're printed on quality cardstock, bundled in box sets, and sold locally and around the state at highway rest stops. The proceeds are used to support the preservation of bird habitats.

Austin's class had loved this project so much that they managed to convince their first-grade teacher to run a similar year-long project, this time about butterflies. Having just seen a western tiger swallowtail fluttering around his backyard, Austin thought it would make an excellent choice for the project. He chose a glossy swallowtail diagram from the pile of butterfly samples on the teacher's desk, got to work on his initial sketch, and drew this:

Not a Rembrandt, but not bad for a six-year-old. Austin's sketch, drawn on lined butcher paper, had managed to capture the swallowtail's basic size and contour. No one would mistake it for a dragonfly or even a fighter jet. Actually, a sketch like this would, in most cases, receive approving marks from the teacher, find its way home to Mom and Dad, and be hung proudly atop the refrigerator for all to see and adore. But not at Anser. At this school, first drafts are never final products. And the revision process isn't just managed by teachers—the students get a say, too.

From the time they enter school, the kids at Anser are taught to critique each other's work in a way that's delicate but detailed. Even at a tender age, they give each other feedback that's focused on the future—not about the work they've done, but about the work that *needs* to get done. So not long after Austin drew his butterfly, a troop of first graders assembled on a brightly colored circle mat, quietly studied his work, and, after a thoughtful silence, began to weigh in.

"It should be pointier," said one boy.

"The legs need to look like triangles," said a girl sitting nearby.

"Where are the swallowtails?" asked a third child, referring to the extensions that should have appeared under the butterfly's wings.

They were right. So Austin went back to work, this time producing a more angular version of his butterfly, complete with swallowtails. Back at the carpet, his classmates noted his improvements but pointed out that it was missing upper and lower wings on both sides. So Austin made a third version, this time with the forgotten pair of wings. His progress from that initial draft was considerable. Notice the distinctive changes in two successive tries:

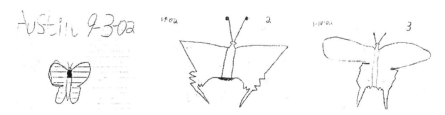

He was getting closer. With a little more angularity, the wings would be set, and Austin could start reproducing the color pattern to get it to match the real thing. He did three more drafts—six in total—before finally earning the enthusiastic approval of his classmates. With each round of feedback, they helped him transform his butterfly, from the initial sketch down to the final rendition—which, by the way, looked so lifelike it could have flapped right off the page.

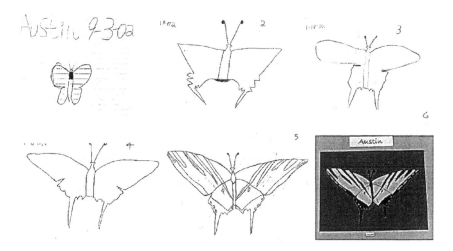

When it comes to feedback, there's a lot to be learned from the story of a little boy and his butterfly, and most of it is probably familiar. The feedback that Austin received seemed to have all the right elements: Specific. Honest. Targeted. Timely. It made allowances for setbacks but didn't compromise on high standards. But none of those qualities by themselves explain why a fidgety first grader would quite literally keep coming back to the drawing board and willingly—even happily—submit to multiple rounds of feedback from peers. There was something about that feedback, something in its trajectory and tone, that made this style stand out from the usual feedback fare. That's how Austin's story ends, but it's where ours begins.

FEAR AND LOATHING

This is a book about giving feedback, but not the kind you've come to know and loathe. Whether it's the feedback we give to employees and coworkers, teachers and students, or family and friends, we have a nagging suspicion that it's ultimately going to fail. And we're right.

According to Columbia University psychologist Kevin Ochsner, people apply just 30 percent of the feedback they receive. The rest is ignored, rejected, stonewalled, or mangled the moment it arrives. Even if they don't dread feedback, the vast majority of people just aren't interested in applying it in their professional or personal lives. If delivering feedback is going to run into that much resistance, sharing it seems like a major waste of time and energy.

Then again, feedback moments happen so frequently, and often when we least expect them, that it's hard to avoid the issue altogether. Feedback is happening all the time: It's the wary look you give to the person standing too close to you in line. Or the angry blares of your horn as you chastise the driver who just cut you off in rush-hour traffic. We give feedback when we write reviews about a product, leave comments about a blog, award stars to our Uber driver, and decide whether to tip the barista at Starbucks. And those aren't theoretical scenarios—I experienced all of them firsthand in the course of twenty-four hours while writing this introduction. Giving feedback isn't just a natural blip in our day. It's an inescapable part of our lives.

What all these examples have in common is a predilection for the *past*. You can't retroactively push that person back in line or stop that car from nearly causing an accident. The review or comments you leave aren't likely to change the way you feel, and the ratings or tips you either give or withhold can't alter the service or product you got or wished you received. The past cannot be changed. What happens there, stays there—and there's not a thing we can do about it, which is why so many people try their hardest to simply avoid giving feedback at all costs—even when that means taking a preemptive strike.

You know those customer-experience surveys that hotels sometimes leave in the rooms? It turns out that travelers are less likely to book return trips to hotels that ask them to rate their stay. The same holds true for supermarkets that pester shoppers about their pre-purchase expectations at the checkout counter. We would rather sleep or shop somewhere else—even if the hotel or supermarket meets all our other consumer criteria—just as long as it means not having to deal with giving feedback about past experiences we can't change or control.

Not only can those feedback encounters be unpleasant, but they can also get downright negative. In the high-stakes testing culture of modern education, schools are allowing grades and performance data to undercut real and meaningful learning. Study after study has found that students—from elementary school to graduate school and across multiple cultures—demonstrate less interest in learning as a result of being graded. Feedback in the form of grades is the ultimate restraint: The grade can't be changed, the lesson can't be relearned, and numbers and letters don't spell out a way forward. Worse, teachers and students get stuck on the wheel of relentless grading, diminished interest in learning, poor outcomes, more tests and grades—the cycle quickly turns vicious. But the real victim is the knowledge that students might have otherwise gained had feedback amounted to more than a rating.

The picture is just as dismal when you move from the classroom to the board room. As chapter 1 explains, the familiar model of performance management is broken. With its lack of frequency, judgmental tone, endless documentation, and uncompromising emphasis on past performance, the "rank and yank" fervor of the last three decades is turning out to be a talent suppressor, not accelerant. Most of the time, feedback comes too late. Managers don't like giving it. Employees don't like getting it. Yet, somehow, a majority of businesses still end up going for it.

Clearly, different people from different places seem to want and need more than traditional feedback can provide. But if that isn't the answer, what is?

FEEDFORWARD: SHIFTING TO FUTURE TENSE

Everyone from chronic dieters to recovering alcoholics knows this fundamental truth about change: You can't kick an old habit until you a form a new one. Fortunately, human beings are remarkably adept at changing and orienting our behavior toward long-term goals and long-term benefits—providing, of course, that we apply enough resolve and repetition along the way. To make meaningful changes in our feedback, it's not enough to simply unlearn the mistakes of the past. We have to actually replace the past with something else.

The future.

It's here, in the shift to future tense, that we place feedback into an entirely different context. In the past, we look back. In the future, we gaze ahead. In the past, we must relive mistakes. In the future, we can reimagine success. The past is a time for reflection. The future is a place for action. The past is already transcribed. The future is still unwritten. We can never change the past. We can always transform the future.

In the past, we gave feedback. In the future, we'll give *feedforward*.

Feedforward is a new approach to performance. It comes from Marshall Goldsmith, one of the world's most successful and admired executive coaches, as a way to help individuals, teams, and organizations achieve a positive change in their behavior. "While they don't particularly like hearing criticism," Goldsmith writes, "successful people love getting ideas for the future." That's because "successful people have a high need for self-determination and are more likely to accept ideas that they 'own,' not those that feel forced upon them."

Feedforward is based on the idea that people develop best when they focus their energy and attention on a future they can change, not on a past they can't. And when we help others make the leap from past to prologue, we give them permission to rewrite their own stories of performance. Gone are the usual elements of judgment, criticism, and appraisal. Instead, feedforward changes the narrative to one of acceptance, support, and development. It supplies others with new ways of thinking about the way they work, learn, and live. Whether these exchanges are taking place between managers and workers, teachers and students, or parents and children, feedforward lets us dump the past, embrace the future, and change the way we lead and live. And that's something that needs to happen right now.

Because unless we fix our feedback, it's going to stay broken.

"REPAIR": SIX TOOLS TO FIX THE FUTURE

The first part of this book talks about The Fix. Chapter 1 shows why traditional feedback needs fixing by taking us inside one of the world's largest professional services companies and showing how it has used feedforward to systematically reimagine the world of performance management. We'll see the emergence of a new workplace ethos that focuses less on numbers and ratings and more on people and process.

Once we learn how to identify feedforward in principle, we have to know how to apply it in practice. That will bring us to chapter 2, where we'll lay out a six-part plan for REPAIR. It stands for:

- Regenerates
- Expands
- Particular
- Authentic
- Impact
- Refines

Each step in REPAIR represents a core component of feedforward. And while they're all mutually enhancing, they don't necessarily need to be practiced in unison. Some high-performing organizations and individuals fully commit to the process of REPAIR; others might choose just a few.

But because performance is rarely an all-or-nothing proposition, feedforward shouldn't be, either. Learning to develop these complex habits takes lots of practice and persistence. It's more like following a sloped curve than taking a sudden plunge. That's why each step in REPAIR comes wrapped in story frames and strategies that make it easier to get going. From a hoops legend to a legendary hospital, we learn that getting what we want means giving others what they need.

Finally, in The Upgrade, we'll explore the way feedforward helps people change the way they lead and live. Operating in the past, traditional feedback acts more like a silencer than an amplifier. The one-way conversations, the generic checklists, the obligatory action items—they all come from a single source: the person giving the feedback, not the one receiving it. But with feedforward, managers and teachers who might ordinarily grab all the airtime learn to hand some of that back to others, causing them to experience a dramatic improvement across four areas of performance and potential:

Creativity

In the information age, when knowledge comes cheap, the real differentiator is how—not what—we learn. As schools and businesses place ever-increasing importance on design thinking and creative work, feedforward can become a crucial driver of discovery. Chapter 3 follows the movements of a hard-core scientist whose psycho-social experiments show that in order for creativity to take hold, we have to learn to let go. And when we release our grip, we unleash the imaginations of everyone around us.

Consciousness

Hearing someone else's feedback can be helpful, but listening to our inner voice can be transformative. In chapter 4, we'll huddle up with a sports psychologist who is turning the world of high performance inside out by reversing the way feedback is shared. From an NFL powerhouse to a retailing giant, feedforward is helping people develop their "inside game" by tapping the self-knowledge they already possess. Turning on our personal channel can improve our performance at work, our relationships with peers, our competitiveness on the field, and even our personal health and well-being. Through self-talk, mindfulness, and five other cognitive habits, feedforward enables us to work smarter, play harder, and live better.

Teams

In today's rapidly changing workplace, feedback is a team sport. Chapter 5 profiles a leading executive coach whose company is changing the bottom line on how big business communicates its higher purpose. Surprisingly, in the context of teams, what we show may be more important than what we say. From monkey brains and peanuts to team dynamics and pizza, feedforward can turn teams into team genius. We'll look at how it unleashes psychological and social ripple effects throughout organizations and explore four strategies for getting teams to communicate and cooperate more effectively using feedforward.

Autonomy

Why do the minority students at one urban school consistently achieve higher graduation rates than their peers? The secret is self-produced. Chapter 6 makes the case for autonomy-supportive feedforward that gives people the confidence and competence to act. We'll present three drivers of autonomy that influence the way we hire and retain talent; develop high performance in schools; and create relationships marked by trust, belonging, and optimism. We'll also expose autonomy killers like praise and incentives and offer three feedforward strategies for getting people to stand up and serve on their own.

The experiences we create for others—success or failure, joy or fear, growth or decline—are formed not just by what we say but also by what they hear. From managers and coaches trying to energize their teams to teachers hoping to motivate their students to parents looking to empower their children, people from all walks of life are searching for the right words, at the right moment, for the right outcomes.

Isn't it time they found them?

■　■　■

Through a lively blend of stories and studies, *The Feedback Fix* shows the power that each of us has to shape human performance and potential. From board rooms to classrooms, and even around dining rooms, feedforward can change the tone and trajectory of everyday communication. People tend to accept feedback that's consistent with the way they see themselves. But with feedforward, we learn to help others see themselves in an entirely new way.

The future is a place of possibility. When we move feedback out of the past and into the future, we start to build a better picture of what others have to say and are able to do. And if we make the right adjustments, chances are they'll want to build alongside us, too.

I

THE FIX

1

Why Traditional Feedback Needs Fixing

There's a quiet revolution brewing inside of 30 Rockefeller Plaza, home to Manhattan's media and business elite. Over the years, 30 Rock has seen its share of insurgents, usurpers, and raiders try to disrupt the old order, but nothing quite like this. What's happening here seems to break all the rules of revolutions. There's no fight over power or profits, no secret plans for takeovers or turnarounds, no armies or militias, no alliances or backroom deals, no visible signs of resistance or conflict. There aren't even two sides to this struggle. For now, it remains a revolution of one—that is, one company: Deloitte.

On the surface, Deloitte looks like any other corporate giant. With more than 250,000 employees around the globe, including almost 70,000 in the United States, it is one of the world's largest professional services networks. Deloitte LLP, the U.S. member firm, posted nearly $15 billion in revenue during the 2014 fiscal year. Its array of financial and advisory services is used by businesses across twenty industries, from energy to manufacturing to the life sciences. And the business itself is highly matrixed, staffed by employees who operate with different skill sets, service lines, and geographic stations. For a company of unusual size and reach, Deloitte doesn't seem all that unusual.

Until now.

Roughly three years ago, in the fall of 2013, Deloitte announced plans to radically restructure its review system. It stopped evaluating its employees on the basis of cascading objectives, multi-rater assessments, and number ratings—the trinity of performance management. Instead of tweaking the system, Deloitte scrapped it down to its studs. By declaring war on the status quo, the company's executive team decided it was time to try a completely different approach to sharing feedback.

Ashley Goodall should know. The silver-tongued Brit, who until recently served as Deloitte's chief learning officer and director of leader development, helped lead the company's charge against traditional feedback. In his role, Goodall managed Deloitte's efforts to develop leaders and innovative new methods of performance management. Trim, with almond-brown hair, Goodall speaks with an English accent that is soothing but steady. At Oxford, he studied music, developing a knack for arranging and playing difficult acoustic pieces.

That experience shaped the way he views people and performance. "All of the things in our professional ecosystem—the way we tell an employee how to work, how to grow, how to lead—all of those things must have some sort of consonance if we're going to do the best possible job," he explains. "We need to start paying better attention to people, not just ratings."

For the better part of three decades, that's exactly *not* how Deloitte operated. Its traditional model of performance management, a series of top-down reviews, was fashioned around the ratings craze of the 1980s. (More on that later.) Managers determined objectives for each of their reports at the beginning of the year. When a project finished—or after every quarter, if projects ran long—they rated employees based on how effectively they had met their goals.

Next, managers noted any instances when employees underperformed. In some cases, employees were already aware of their mistakes, but that knowledge was never guaranteed. More often than not, missteps only came to light during the review itself, not in the moment of error. So instead of addressing problems in real time, managers quietly noted them in a personnel file and moved on. Now, months later, they looked back at these events from the rearview mirror, trying from afar to recall what they saw.

Finally, these batched evaluations were factored into a single year-end rating, reached in lengthy consensus meetings at which groups of "counselors" discussed hundreds of people in light of their peers. Depending on the rating each employee received, he or she would be tracked for promotion, bumped up the pay scale, or flagged for probation. The most glaring underperformers—those with the lowest ratings—faced termination.

The process seemed way too forensic—re-creating past performance based on shreds of evidence—and felt strangely outmoded by twenty-first-century standards. "The traditional model worked very well when business measured a person's output," Goodall observed. "It was born in an industrial age when we could count how many bricks you laid or railroad ties you installed. Now all of that's changed."

WHY IT FAILS

Business in the twenty-first century looks nothing like it did one hundred years ago. Today, more than 70 percent of all employees work in service- or knowledge-related jobs. Their performance is powered by their technical know-how and ability to innovate by working in teams. Learning the right skills is just a matter of having the right kind of training. But applying those skills in the highly complex world of teams requires the right kind of development. And since no project ever goes completely according to plan—there's the inevitable course correction in strategy, objectives, or personnel—it makes you wonder: Instead of ranking people's capabilities at a single moment in time, wouldn't it make more sense to gradually nurture and refine them *over time*?

Then there's the problem of variability, or what researchers have dubbed the "idiosyncratic rater effect." Imagine yourself in one of Deloitte's year-end consensus meetings, when managers render decisions about employees' work. Sealed off from the rest of the group, an internal team of Deloitte counselors pours over a caseload of one hundred employees—say, from the audit division. Like archeologists on a dig, they furiously sift through batches of project summaries and end-of-quarter reports issued by managers to piece together the strengths and weaknesses of each employee.

And then the unavoidable happens. As they begin to evaluate performance, counselors filter the data through their own mental dashboards—the deep-seated, highly distinct set of prior assumptions, beliefs, and predispositions they've formed over their lifetimes. This shield acts like a cognitive compass that guides and directs their review process. There's nothing inherently wrong with following the familiar. But when instincts mix with information, the result can be misleading.

That's because each reviewer's field of view becomes clouded by personal idiosyncrasies. In an instant, the ability to objectively study and evaluate information is overtaken by some personal feeling or experience from the past. Without realizing it, the raters may draw completely different conclusions about the same set of data on the basis of certain triggers or cues. Everyone in the group sets out to reach the same destination but ends up following different coordinates. They can't help it—they're navigating with bias.

Consider a recent study of nearly forty-five hundred managers who were evaluated on certain performance dimensions by two bosses, two peers, and two subordinates. The six-member team produced highly variable ratings of the managers, but only 21 percent of those differences could be attributed to *actual* events. An astounding 62 percent of the variance resulted from the priority and consideration given by raters to certain performance metrics. When it came to giving the ratings, some actions mattered more than others, and they differed from one rater to the next.

Or, to put it more bluntly: The feedback said more about the person giving the rating than the one receiving it.

Clearly, there was a strong scientific case against the use of ratings. But the wildest revelation—and the one that set the revolution in motion—came when Deloitte actually started crunching the numbers. (That's their business, after all.) Between completing forms, holding meetings, and creating ratings, the company had spent nearly *two million hours a year* on performance management. Besides for the obvious loss of productivity, the system seemed ill suited to address a host of "people issues" like employee engagement, talent development, and career counseling, which is where performance really thrives.

Goodall winces at remembering what the company had unearthed. "As we studied how those hours were spent, we realized that many of them were eaten up by leaders' discussions behind closed doors about the outcomes of the process," he said. "We wondered if we could somehow shift our investment of time from talking to ourselves about ratings to talking to our people about their performance and careers." What they needed—and eventually adopted—was a pivot from the past to the future.

STUCK IN REVERSE

The Deloitte discovery shows why traditional feedback needs fixing. In searching for a way forward, the company recognized it could no longer afford to look back, which is what usually happens with most feedback. When we talk about things that belong to the past, the conversation stalls. No one can go back in time and write a different outcome. What's done is done. And that's why traditional feedback is fundamentally flawed: It's supposed to bring change, but people can't change what they can't control.

Giving feedback to others about things they can't change is like asking them to step out from a block of cement that has already set. That might have worked before, while the compound was still wet, but not now. People don't get a redo on the past, so telling them about their mistakes after the fact will only bring helplessness and frustration. Had they known sooner, these individuals might have handled each situation differently.

But it's not just a problem of bad timing. Delivering feedback in past tense often comes across as judgmental. Because traditional feedback is usually shared by a supervisor, it heightens sensitivities and puts people on high alert. They become defensive. Even innocent observations about performance can read like harsh accusations. It feels like a trial—and in many ways, it is: Feedback subjects us to the court of public opinion, even if that opinion just belongs to one other person.

Scientists have picked up on this phenomenon as well. New brain research shows that certain regions of the mind go dark when our status is threatened—something that can often happen in the course of a performance review, especially if we're told that we're not making the cut. What happens next is a sort of mental paralysis: The neurotransmitters in our brains that help us carry out executive functions become dull and lifeless. That, in turn, constricts our fields of view, making it harder for us to take in information, process data, and unleash creativity. While negative feedback isn't all bad— we'll see why in the next chapter—it has the potential to throw our brains into survival mode, as stress-inducing hormones flood our neural pathways.

That causes a dismal effect on the psyche of the person receiving feedback. People tend to believe the things they're told by a boss or trusted colleague, even if the message isn't one they'd like to hear. So when feedback is especially brutal and deeply rooted in the past, people tend to adopt a fixedly dim view of their capabilities and fall victim to "learned helplessness," a psychological condition that causes people to act helplessly, even when they have the power to change their debilitating state of mind.

With so many strikes against it, traditional feedback is starting to lose its luster among the managing class. In fact, managers may even dislike giving feedback more than employees dislike receiving it. In surveys of managers and human resource professionals, leadership advisory firm CEB found that only 23 percent responded favorably to their company's current performance management practices. That's a steep decline from a decade ago, when the satisfaction rate stood at 50 percent.

Since 2013, 85 percent of HR managers surveyed have either made changes in hopes of improvement or plan to do so in coming years. Those changes may take years to materialize, but, in the meantime, it's pretty clear that the status quo isn't drawing rave reviews.

Let's sum up. So far, we've described five ways that traditional feedback needs fixing. When we share it, people tend not to hear us. This is because:

1. **It consumes too much time and productivity.** By its own estimate, Deloitte was spending almost 2 million hours per year on traditional reporting—the equivalent of 547 working hours in a single day.

2. **It focuses on the past, which can't be changed.** We resist the change we can't control. And we can't control the past—we can only live with it and hopefully learn from it.

3. **It comes across as judgmental.** It doesn't matter if the feedback comes from a parent, a teacher, or a boss. As long as there's hierarchy, we feel like someone is handing down a sentence.

4. **It perpetuates negative behaviors and beliefs.** Hearing about our flaws leads to the debilitating experience of learned helplessness, which prevents us from grasping the solutions readily available to us.

5. **It diminishes the prospect of growth.** The self-defeating tone of traditional feedback pins people to an unchanging narrative about their own intelligence and abilities.

So if traditional feedback is so flawed, how come it continues to occupy our workplaces, schools, and homes?

Strange as it sounds, it started with factory lighting.

FEEDBACK: A SHORT HISTORY

The first time performance reviews received serious consideration dates back to the 1930s, when a Harvard Business School professor named Elton Mayo studied the behavior of workers at the Hawthorne Works, a large factory complex of the Western Electric Company in Cicero, Illinois, just a short drive from Chicago's urban hub. During its heyday in the first half of the twentieth century, the Hawthorne Works housed more than forty-five thousand employees and produced large quantities of telephone equipment and other consumer goods, such as refrigerators and electric fans.

Managers at the Hawthorne Works commissioned Mayo and several colleagues to observe the effects of industrial conditions on worker productivity. In one series of tests, the team discovered that intermittent changes in lighting intensity inside the plant produced a temporary boost in worker performance. In another study, Mayo found that workers who assembled telephone relays produced double their typical output when allowed to choose their own teammates and retreat to a "special" work room fifty or so feet from their usual spot on the factory floor.

The experiments ran over the course of five years. After combing through all the observations, exit interviews, and data samples, Mayo concluded that workers tended to enjoy short-lived boosts in performance when they felt that managers paid attention to them, a phenomenon that later came to be known as the "Hawthorne effect." Degrees of happiness and productivity, the theory went, correlated directly to the social structure of the workplace.

Workers seemed to crave the empathetic recognition of their employers—regardless of whether their bosses actually liked them. An attentive boss meant a more engaged employee. Even trivial gestures like brightening the factory floor provided a measure of comfort for workers, who, in turn, responded by producing better work. They just needed to feel like they were being noticed.

Suddenly, it wasn't enough to simply hire someone to do a job; bosses had to manage and mentor people, too. That usually happened in formal meetings, a time when managers could review procedures, talk about company business, or just rally the troops. In 1950, these interactions became enshrined in corporate culture with the passage of the Performance Rating Act, which mandated annual reviews of all federal employees. Subsequent legislation would tie bonuses and salaries to these assessments. Soon, the private sector followed with its own set of review reforms.

The performance management movement was born.

But it wasn't until 1981 that the framework we know today as traditional feedback took hold throughout the American workplace. That was the year Jack Welch became the chief executive of GE, beginning an iconic twenty-year run as America's most celebrated corporate leader. Welch pioneered the "rank and yank" approach to employee review, a three-step ratings scale that measured individual goals and performance on a bell curve. The top 15 percent of performers were awarded a 1; the middle 70 percent were assigned a 2; and the bottom 15 percent were designated a 3. The 1s got promoted ("ranked"). The 3s got canned ("yanked").

Wooed by GE's success—at one point, it was the highest-valued American company at $300 billion—other companies quickly adopted "rank and yank" in their own management ecosystems. By 2012, nearly 60 percent of Fortune 500 companies used some version of it, just with more euphemistic titles like "talent assessment" or "performance procedure." Apparently, calling it "rank and yank" engendered about as much excitement around the office as mandatory drug testing.

And so the top-down, rear-facing process of giving feedback developed, unchecked, for much of the late twentieth century. What began as an earnest attempt to apply industrial research morphed in a systematic reduction of employees to numbers, efforts to ratings, and managers to bean counters. Something had to change. The entire enterprise needed a switch. For that, we return to Deloitte.

THINKING IN THE FUTURE TENSE

"We've arrived at a very different and much simpler design for managing people's performance," promises Ashley Goodall, the former Deloitte learning chief. It's designed to accelerate performance, not slow it down. "The first thing we do is help people pay attention to their experiences at work—the things that lift them up and the things that push them down." As a launch point for reflection, team members use a self-assessment tool to diagnose their strengths. This mirror-holding exercise gives employees insight into their professional capacities—the core of who they are.

The next step is to uncover who they want to *become*. Team members are encouraged to convene weekly "check-ins" with their team leader to receive near-future communications about upcoming assignments, expectations for the coming week, or comments about recently completed work. The power of these interactions—a team leader's "killer app," according to Goodall—lies in their simplicity: More frequent contact within a team's ranks allows people to nimbly shift priorities and realign expectations based on a steady stream of communication.

But at their core, these check-ins are instruments of development, not evaluation. They are designed to spark conversations between team leaders and members about individual strengths, team goals, and future aspirations.

During a check-in, the team leader might offer guidance to a team member on how to handle client relations differently, creating an opening to discuss other barriers that stand in the way of achieving better end results. The fluid nature of check-ins makes talent development a more natural and ongoing part of the employee experience, one that Deloitte hopes will lead to greater engagement and better performance outcomes. (More on that in chapter 2.)

Deloitte has also replaced its batched system of year-end performance reviews with a more real-time outlook of employee work. Known internally as "performance snapshots," these at-a-glance reports are intended to assemble a current profile of each member's critical skills, behaviors, and dispositions. Managers still compile this data after every project or quarter, but with one radical difference: They aren't assessing past work but *future prospects*.

Again, there's a premium on simplicity. Instead of drawing upon the usual set of cascading targets, managers create performance snapshots around four basic questions about the employee, listed in the table on the next page. Note the language of each question, how it is rated, and the information it is designed to reveal.

By design, only managers with deep knowledge of the employee produce the snapshots—not former supervisors, colleagues from other departments, or even members from the same team. On the question of who is best suited to evaluate performance, Deloitte believes that the people who are closest to the action have the clearest view. In tightening the feedback loop, the company hopes to amplify performance knowledge through one voice, not many.

Radical Redesign: Deloitte's Performance Snapshot

(1) Given what I know of this person's performance, and if it were my money, I would award this person the highest possible compensation increase and bonus.	Rated on a five-point scale [from "strongly agree" to "strongly disagree"]	Measures overall performance and unique value to the organization
(2) Given what I know of this person's performance, I would always want him or her on my team.	Rated on a five-point scale [from "strongly agree" to "strongly disagree"]	Measures ability to work well with others
(3) This person is at risk for low performance.	Yes/No	Identifies problems that might harm the customer or team
(4) This person is ready for promotion today.	Yes/No	Identifies employee's potential

But what about the tendency of managers to deliver feedback with blinders on—the "idiosyncratic rater effect" described earlier? Goodall thinks they have the answer. "People may rate other people's skills inconsistently, but they are highly consistent when rating their own feelings and intentions," he said. "In effect, we are asking our team leaders what they would *do* with each team member, rather than what they *think* of that individual."

That's a major departure from traditional feedback systems that, as we've seen, operate backward and leave very little room for employee participation. Not here. In its total form, the Deloitte model upends all the assumptions of traditional feedback—from basic functions like how to gather and share information to more complex foundations like the purpose and potential of talent management. It moves from a parochial focus on numbers and ratings to a panoramic view of people and process.

The company's road to reinvention cuts through the narrowness of traditional feedback. Rather than dwell in the past, managers speak into the future by allowing larger conversations about work and career to unfold—the beginnings of feedforward. From a development standpoint, that's far more appealing and productive than the once-a-year reporting that feels more like a seasonal sport, a backward contest that picks winners and losers on the basis of retrospect, long after the game has ended.

LOOKING FORWARD, NOT BACK

Reimagined performance management can lead employees down a path of self-discovery, professional clarity, and personal growth. It produces the fullest value of every individual. It promotes clarity over intuition. Most important, it brings into the conversation the person most responsible for producing meaningful change: the employee. When that happens, the result is transformative. Instead of managing other people's performance, we develop their talent. We start to turn feedback into feedforward.

Judging by the number of high-profile companies who have joined the movement, Deloitte won't be pressing along alone for much longer. Microsoft made waves when it recently announced that it would abandon its legacy practice of stack rankings, a throwback to the "rank and yank" era. Adobe, Gap, and Medtronic have embraced the notion of a weekly "check-in" between team leaders and members. Accenture, the professional services firm with over three hundred thousand employees worldwide, is abolishing annual reviews altogether. The same goes for Cargill and Juniper Systems. And the list continues to grow.

■ ■ ■

This is not just a business objective. Giving better feedback is a *people* objective. It's the way teachers get more from their students, parents get more from their children, and all of us get more from our friends, colleagues, and loved ones. But as we said in the introduction, *getting what we want means giving others what they need.* People don't need feedback that passes judgment, reinforces negativity, takes too much time, and always—*always*—looks back on a past that can't be changed, not a future that can.

What we need is something completely different: a system of feedback that helps people find their inner voice, discover their natural creativity, strengthen their significance, and stand on their own two feet. In other words, we need *feedforward*—the future-leaning feedback that creates consciousness, unleashes creativity, repurposes teams, and builds autonomy and resilience. Each of these qualities will be explored in part II of this book.

But for now, we need to identify the essential elements of feedforward to see how it works in practice. The six-point plan—we call it REPAIR for short—can make a dramatic difference in our interactions at work, school, and life. Each part can help fix the way we conduct everyday conversations with the people closest to us. The next chapter shows us how.

2

Feedforward

Six Tools to REPAIR the Future

1. REGENERATES

Mike Preston will forgive you for thinking it's a high-end resort. That's the first thing that comes to mind when you stand in the lobby of Deloitte University, the sprawling, state-of-the-art leadership and training facility located some sixteen hundred miles from the firm's corporate headquarters at 30 Rock.

While you're there, you can work out with personal trainers in a twelve-thousand-square-foot fitness center, dine on exotic international cuisine prepared by world-class chefs, stroll along a two-mile trail lined by rolling hills and native prairie grasses, listen to top-rate presenters at the massive 176-seat indoor amphitheater, and catch live music after hours at the Barn, a woodsy meeting spot. The only thing you won't do is bother with reservations—or a wallet, for that matter. From end to end, it's all free.

Spread across 107 acres of cattle ranching land in Texas Hill Country, the $300 million facility, completed in 2011, is a rustic but gleaming destination for Deloitte employees to learn, grow, and relax. Visitors can stay in any of the eight hundred well-appointed guest rooms that offer plush amenities and clever features suggested by Deloitte employees, like reading lights installed over headboards and shower handles placed on the wall opposite the nozzle so guests don't get wet turning it on. "Not the Four Seasons," quips Preston, Deloitte's chief talent officer for U.S. firms and my guide for the day. "But they're quite nice."

Creature comforts aside, Deloitte University—or DU, as people here like to call it—offers a dynamic learning environment as well. There are thirty-three high-tech classrooms with integrated audiovisual equipment, including four telerooms that link up to Deloitte sites across the United States and around the world. Spaces are designed to allow for lots of different learning configurations, from large-group presentations and lectures to small-group study and private meetings. If your team is looking to solve a particularly knotty problem, they might escape to the Greenhouse, a Zen-inspired innovation hub where new ideas get pitched and launched. Executives reserve space upstairs in the second-floor conference area, complete with high-definition videoconferencing and an outdoor patio suite that overlooks the pristine grounds.

More than sixty-five thousand employees from cross-functional teams spend time at DU each year, including all of the firm's new hires, as well as team leaders celebrating career milestones or senior-level appointments. "We imagined an environment that would drive leadership development and would bring together varying perspectives and expertise about our core businesses," says Preston as we walk past a twenty-foot-long media wall that gives a digital rundown of DU events and company information. "It's a place where our people can go to learn, refresh, and recharge, but more importantly, interact with one another while experiencing our company's culture firsthand."

Just how to communicate that culture—parts of which were chronicled in the last chapter—wasn't immediately clear. Within Deloitte, partners debated the merits of "bricks versus clicks"—investing in physical space or technological infrastructure—and ultimately decided on bricks. The result was Deloitte University, which opened in October 2011 with the goal of growing leadership skill at every level of the organization. The world-class campus is unlike any of Deloitte's other offices or development centers around the world. Despite its colossal size—it stands at more than seven hundred thousand square feet—DU seems more like a town square than a corporate hub, though with a distinctively global feel.

What at first appears to be a company getaway is really a destination for talent development. It showcases Deloitte's commitment to boosting engagement across four domains—inclusion, well-being, development, and impact—and creating a dynamic learning environment for growth and mobility. Amid all the perks and frills, the premise of DU is remarkably simple: Talent needs to be treated as an investment, not an expense. Helping people find the right mix of passion, purpose, and performance is how organizations grow their talent and create staying power for the long term.

It's no secret that the rising class of millennials wants more from work than work itself. They're searching for personal meaning alongside professional fulfillment. According to one recent survey, employees hold work passion to be twice as important as career ambition, weighing factors like company mission, values, and work-life integration when choosing a new job or staying with the one they have. For younger workers especially, the goal isn't just climbing the ladder but also balancing out the rungs—getting ahead without leaving behind life's other pursuits.

This new reality is why the first part of the REPAIR plan—the one where talent Regenerates—is a must-do for employers seeking to attract and retain their best prospects. In an open-talent economy, where globalization and mobility have made it easier for workers to slide between roles or even change jobs completely, employers have to grow talent to keep it. For many workers, especially millennials, the name of the game isn't lifetime employment but employability—reaping skills and opportunities that lead to job rotation, accelerated leadership, and ongoing improvement. At a time when short-term gigs are becoming the new career, it's a good bet that talent will flow to places where dynamic learning—marked by strong and continuous feedback—sits high atop the culture chain.

When feedforward Regenerates talent, it sets the conditions that allow people to become more engaged in their work. At the simplest level, it leads to the unmistakable feeling that we're moving forward in our professional and personal lives. Getting positive feedback about our performance may feel good, but it doesn't break new ground. It merely confirms what we already know about ourselves and our talents, essentially holding our growth in check. But when feedback gets us thinking about how to spread that talent to others, it has a multiplying effect. We make our talent a source and force for growth all around us.

As people make the shift from talent hoarders to talent producers, they end up growing through giving. Take this scenario: A school administrator tells a highly rated and respected teacher, "You know, you do a great job organizing class projects." That's nice to hear, maybe even validating—but also self-evident. The teacher, no stranger to these skills, has called upon those traits before and will likely do so again. All the feedback did was confirm a known talent. It did not grow it.

Now reimagine that piece of feedback, this time with a feedforward approach: The administrator would say, "You know, you do a great job organizing class projects. Have you ever considered leading a session about this at our next staff training?" That's not just a comfy pat on the back. It's a full-throated call to action. Instead of letting feedback cushion the talent, it grows it with a bit of a push. And that's when the opportunity for engagement really begins.

Sometimes growth follows a vertical path, leading to a promotion or new position. But it can be horizontal, too, like getting a professional opportunity related to a personal strength, or acquiring new knowledge or skills that lead to better work. James Avey and his colleagues call this "psychological ownership" and have shown that engagement levels are much higher among employees who feel empowered at work and claim ownership over their jobs. These people don't seek advancement—at least not in the conventional sense. They are quite happy to go along filling their professional buckets with growth opportunities that improve their job experience and bring them personal satisfaction.

That's especially true for younger workers just setting out. According to a report by Quantum Workplace, employees under the age of twenty-five rate professional development as their number one driver of engagement, and it remains a top consideration all the way up to the age of thirty-five. Putting feedback into a broader category of career growth makes people feel like their talents are being groomed, not just consumed. After all, there's a reason why schools and corporations call it professional *development*: It develops a stronger sense of who we are and what we can do.

Getting people more engaged in their work comes at a crucial time. The 2016 Global Human Capital Trends report, a survey of seven thousand human resources and business leaders from 130 countries, revealed that nine in ten executives rate engagement as an "important" or "very important" priority for their companies. This follows on the heels of the 2015 report, which showed that 79 percent of businesses are seriously worried about engagement and retention, while two-thirds of business leaders cite "the overwhelmed employee" as a top business challenge.

There's good cause for concern. According to research conducted by Gallup across 142 countries, only 13 percent of employees reported feeling "highly engaged" at work. While at first that might not seem terribly ominous, it's the equivalent of 1 in 8 workers—roughly 180 million employees in the countries studied—who don't feel psychologically committed to their jobs or who are unlikely to make positive contributions to their organizations. That's a lot of people who are checked out even before they clock in for the day.

But even problems of enormous scale can be solved through gradual culture shifts. By putting employee engagement at the forefront, we help people discover the best versions of themselves at work and give them reasons to stay. It's not enough to gauge employee engagement once a year through surveys; by the time the results roll in, attitudes have already hardened and set. Instead, employers must *proactively* develop talent with opportunities for continuous learning, professional growth, and work-life balance.

That's what Deloitte realized when it created DU and why other organizations are starting to treat engagement as a core business strategy. The nature of work might change, but human nature does not. People want to do meaningful work, receive valuable feedback about their performance, and make forward progress in their careers. When we draw out the burgeoning potential of every individual, we not only grow talent—we keep it, too.

Fast Fix: Feedforward **Regenerates** Talent   REPAIR

1. To attract and retain top prospects, organizations must treat talent as an investment, not an expense.
2. The most enduring companies and organizations create opportunities for accelerated leadership, job rotation, and continuous improvement.
3. Not everyone is looking for advancement. At certain points in their careers, some people are looking to move horizontally.

2. EXPANDS

Pixar is one of the most successful movie studios in Hollywood. Over the years, it has collected more than twenty Academy Awards for hits like *Toy Story*, *The Incredibles*, and *Finding Nemo*, and its last eight films have grossed more than $500 million worldwide. The memorable characters and storylines that Pixar dreams up have delighted moviegoers of all ages. But behind the box office magic is an active feedback system that's built on candor, openness, and a willingness to reimagine—again and again.

Creating full-length animated films is definitely not child's play. A single scene lasting just four seconds requires about one hundred frames, which can take up to a week to produce. For the 2001 smash *Monsters, Inc.*, animators spent twelve hours on each frame, many of which featured Sully, the film's furry blue hero, and his 2,320,413 individually animated hairs, each painstakingly created to appear like the real thing.

During the early stages of animation, each animator works on one or two scenes at a time, then feeds drafts into a central computer, where they are reviewed by supervising animators and the film's director. Everything in a scene—from the placement of a prop to the way a character's eyes roll—is carefully vetted and scrutinized.

Any changes in animation may require adjustments to a character's rig, or the digital dimensions that shape facial expressions and body movements. Rigging is a complex web of formulas, coding, and physics, and any imprecision in the rig can compromise a character's lifelike performance on-screen. It's challenging enough to create the actual sculptures, called maquettes, which become the basis for three-dimensional imaging. But trying to digitize the physical world raises the complexity to a whole new level.

Imagine this: According to the latest scientific estimates, humans are capable of making about twenty facial expressions, but Pixar's animators can achieve nearly thirty times that expressive range—about seven hundred shades of the most basic emotions. The technology is astounding, but so is the potential drag. Even a minor change in a facial detail can cause a major ripple effect down the production chain.

By the time the action moves toward modeling and simulation, every aspect of the story—from camera angles and lighting to sound effects and motion capture—is reviewed and revised. Story artists, film editors, technical directors, and creative designers continue to make changes to bits and pieces of the film as it travels down the pipeline. All that trimming adds up. In Pixar's latest sensation, *Inside Out*, more than 146,000 images were scoped for the final cut. The maquette for the main character, Joy, changed seventeen times before designers settled on the right look.

Working in an environment with constant revision cycles can be frustrating, even for the process-loving creatives that Pixar tends to employ. When the animation team assembles for the daily "crit session"—the fateful moment when the previous day's work gets dissected—there's no guarantee a scene will make the final cut. One by one, animators take turns scrutinizing each other's creative interpretations, second-guessing and debating ideas that until now seemed pretty solid. What emerges is a sharper and more refined version of the feed—some of it familiar, but most of it transformed.

But verbal sparring does not by itself produce better animatics. The reason these crit sessions are so effective—and a major reason Pixar continues to churn out one blockbuster after the next—is because animators are just as quick to raise possibilities as they are to topple them. They aren't allowed to shoot down ideas unless they can propose workable alternatives, a phenomenon the studio likes to call "plussing," since it forces the idea count up, not down. Rather than reject a concept entirely, animators accept its premise but add on suggestions for improvement.

In practice, it might go something like this: Animators for the upcoming *Toy Story 4* review a storyboard with the creative director at a crit session. The director might say, "I like Woody's eyes, but what if they rolled left?" This is a classic plussing technique. The director accepts the premise of the sketch (Woody's expression), identifies a potential flaw (the way his eyes slant), and adds a productive alternative (tweak them to the left). The statement is matter-of-fact, brutally honest, and nonjudgmental. No one, not the director or the animator, is left wondering what needs to happen next.

It also stimulates more thinking. With just two small words—*what if*—the feedback giver challenges the receiver to reconsider the concept, imagine an alternative, and create a better version than the one he had before. Instead of leaving people stranded at a dead end, plussing helps them think about ways to turn the corner. And with its idea-generating approach, Pixar demonstrates the second feedforward fix: Expands.

When we deliver feedback in a way that expands thinking, we show the power of *more*. More leverage over options. More room for creativity. More control over process. We get people to stop seeing what is and start imagining what *can be*.

Just because we're selective about the feedback we choose to share doesn't mean we should limit where it leads. That's the essential point of plussing—to offer feedback that keeps ideas flowing, which, if done well, carries a huge upside: When there's no cap on possibilities, there's no limit on progress.

With any sort of creative work—painting a portrait, composing a sonata, or writing a book—people inevitably run into a wall. After hours of staring at the same canvas, pouring over the same melody, or fixating on the same paragraph, it's hard to imagine what something might look like beyond its current form. But with feedforward that Expands, people suddenly develop a knack for details and direction they never had before. A tweak in color, a change in measure, a shift in word choice and tone—the small adjustments that come from plussing unlock dramatic improvements in performance, so long as we're willing to see these idea shapers as aggregators, not adversaries.

Among the team at Pixar, where collaboration runs high, there is a strong inclination toward feedback that is additive, not competitive. Ed Catmull, the company's cofounder and president, sums it up this way: "A competitive approach measures other ideas against your own, turning the discussion into a debate about who won and lost. An additive approach, on the other hand, starts with the understanding that each participant contributes something to the discussion."

It helps, of course, to work on a team that operates with a high level of mutual respect and trust. Hashing out ideas and submitting to critiques is a lot easier when everyone sitting around the table is collegial. But even if your team isn't exactly Pixar-esque, you can ease into plussing by using a particular set of language that raises people's thinking quotient instead of lowering it. It divides into two distinct language types we'll call *amplifiers* and *silencers*. They act as opposites, and understanding their effect on creative thinking could very well determine whether feedback expands possibilities, as the nearby table shows.

Could the tone be any more different? Silencers are closed and negative. They feature words like *but, never, don't,* and *aren't*—language that is restrictive, dismissive, and disapproving. Silencers close the door on other people's ideas. If you try plussing with a silencer, the process won't go very far because it shuts down the process of thinking. On the other end, you have amplifiers, which sound more open and positive. They communicate in a way that's flexible, encouraging, and agreeable. Amplifiers keep the lights on upstairs. If you try plussing with an amplifier, chances are you'll be successful since it lobs ideas up the thinking chain.

Silencers (–)	Amplifiers (+)
"Yes, but . . ."	"Yes, and . . ."
"That will never work."	"What if we tried this?"
"I don't see that happening."	"How might we do this?"
"We aren't staffed for that."	"Let's try to reallocate."

When we find the right words to fix feedback, the constructive conflict that emerges leads to better thinking that's also longer lasting. That's what researchers found when they challenged three groups of participants to come up with a way to ease traffic congestion in San Francisco, ranked among U.S. cities as the second-worst place to drive, costing riders an average of nearly six days in lost time due to commuting delays. (Los Angeles takes the top prize, but not by much.)

The first group, the study's control, received no further instructions and was told to devise as many solutions as possible. The second group—let's call them the "brainstormers"—stuck to the usual brainstorming format, but researchers asked them to withhold any judgment or criticism during the process. The third group—they'll go by the name "debaters"—followed the same format, but with a twist: The researchers not only allowed group members to debate but also *encouraged* it. The brainstormers were told to handle each other with kid gloves. The debaters were allowed to take the gloves off completely.

Not only did the debaters generate 25 percent more ideas than the other two groups, but they also continued to propose solutions even after the group was disbanded. In a follow-up questionnaire, members of that group continued to propose an average of seven traffic solutions, compared to an average of only one to two new ideas from the brainstormers. Researchers attributed their sustained interest in problem solving to the stern but structured nature of their debate, which forced individual members to think hard about their positions and be prepared to actively defend them.

Unlike traditional brainstorming, with its polite and glossy view of all sides, rough-and-tumble debate pokes and tugs at undisciplined ideas until they form something more coherent and whole. There may be a lesson here for managing the flow of ideas in groups of all types and across all settings: If we want to deliver feedforward that expands thinking, having structured debates like those at Pixar may generate more useful and creative ideas than freewheeling brainstorms. The more we fight for ideas on their merits, the better they'll become.

> **Fast Fix:** Feedforward **Expands** Possibilities
>
> 1. Plussing grows ideas by adding on to them.
> 2. Use amplifiers, not silencers, to stimulate creative thinking.
> 3. With groups, try structured debate over brainstorming.

3. PARTICULAR

By anyone's count, Kobe Bryant is a basketball god. The man they call "Black Mamba" spent his twenty-year run with the Los Angeles Lakers spinning and slicing his way through opponents like his venomous moniker. On the court, Bryant collected honors the way some people collect credit card points: quickly, efficiently, and in vast amounts. He led the NBA in scoring for two seasons and ranks third on both the league's all-time regular season and post-season scoring lists.

His legendary achievements include a league-best eighteen trips to the All-Star game, twelve All-Defensive team selections, the most points scored in a single game, and a record fifteen appearances on the All-NBA team—and that's before you start counting the five championship rings. When Bryant laced up for the last time on April 13, 2016, he was cheered on by a capacity crowd of 18,997 at the Staples Center in downtown Los Angeles, and another 5.2 million people watching at home on primetime television. For much of his career, he was immortal.

But there's one stat that goes mostly unnoticed in Bryant's spectacular record: player mentor. After undergoing season-ending shoulder surgery in 2015 to repair a torn rotator cuff, Bryant could have used rehab as a way to retreat. Instead, he took to the sidelines and started mentoring the younger players on the team. "I help them, mentor them, and give them advice," Bryant said, "because I've pretty much seen it all."

Working with up-and-coming stars like D'Angelo Russell and Julius Randle, Bryant turned the bench into his personal academy. For former Lakers coach Byron Scott, who had a front-row seat for Bryant's second act, it was like watching the basketball version of the Last Lecture: "I think he enjoys seeing these guys develop, because in the back of his mind somewhere he looks at them and remembers when he was in that position. I think he enjoys the process of watching these guys grow."

But instead of dumping decades of accumulated wisdom on each player, Bryant took a more selective approach. For shooting guard Wayne Ellington, he outlined what he called "little tricks" that made it easier to move and shoot more efficiently off the screen. During time-outs, Bryant took out a clipboard to diagram various pick-and-roll coverages to help rookie guard Jordan Clarkson find an open shot. With rookie center Tarik Black, he showed him how to develop better footwork and slow down his drives to the hoop to allow his teammates better penetration in the paint.

For the better part of that season, Bryant, who had just turned thirty-seven, played the part of the wise old man to a group of rookies so young they could have been his teenage children. Being the elite that he was, the hard part wasn't knowing what to say—it was deciding what *not* to say. Having perfected his game on both sides of the ball, Bryant could have easily unloaded a sweeping critique of the players' flaws and missteps, but that never happened. His feedback was precise, tailored to individual needs, and decidedly particular—yet another part of the REPAIR plan.

Giving feedback that is Particular is an exercise in restraint. Instead of trying to rearrange the entire picture, we limit ourselves to just a few frames. Like a triage center, feedback is vetted and ordered by priority, treating some issues now and holding others for later. That doesn't mean tuning out the big picture. We still try to identify, communicate, and correct problems as we see them. But instead of casting a wide net over multiple issues, we resolve to capture just a few.

At first, this may seem counterintuitive. People can't fix what they don't know—so holding back information about their performance feels wrong, like we're depriving them of needed information. But when we pick and choose what to say and share, we give more than we take. Since there's a cap on how much anyone can absorb at once, limiting the flow of feedback allows for slower thinking, greater clarity, and—most important—fewer decisions. Because if there's anything that holds people back from making progress, it's having to make decisions.

As we continuously deliberate over new information pouring in throughout the day, our brain space becomes overloaded. That's what Angelika
Dimoka, director of the Center for Neural Decision Making at Temple University, found when she and a team of economists and computer scientists
looked at the effects of "combinatorial auctions"—highly complex bidding
wars where lots of different items can be purchased either alone or in bundles.
The more information bidders had to simultaneously juggle, the more prone
they became to overpaying or committing a mental lapse. Like a circuit
breaker, the overstimulated brain eventually trips off, which is when "people
start making stupid mistakes and bad choices," Dimoka says, "because the
brain region responsible for smart decision making has essentially left the
premises."

Pushing too much information across people's dashboards at once leaves
them in a frenzied state of mind. Instead of providing clarity and direction,
catch-all feedback serves up a hot mess of confusion and ambiguity. Even if
they can somehow cut through the mental clutter and define the goals, coming up with an action plan can feel overwhelming. Work down the list item by
item? Make the easy fixes first before moving on to more complex tasks? It's
challenging enough to go from feedback to follow-through. It's even harder
when you have to decide where to start.

That has to do with something psychologists call "decision fatigue." The
more we decide, the less patient and prudent we become. So when we force
people to juggle lots of decisions rather than handle just a few, their choices
can get sloppy and compromised—and the consequences can be serious.
Take the case of eight Israeli judges tasked with hearing parole requests. With
twenty-two years on average of judicial experience, the judges were anything
but rocky. But when researchers pored over eleven hundred of the board's
decisions made in one year, they found an unusual trend: When appeals
were heard in the morning, the court granted parole in nearly 70 percent of
the cases but paroled less than 10 percent of cases that were heard late in the
afternoon.

By that time, the judges might have listened to nearly forty appeals, each
lasting upward of six minutes. The researchers concluded that these trends—
which didn't result from bias or an unconscious "quota" for favorable rul-
ings—came down to a simple fact: The judges were flat-out tired of making

decisions. And like anyone suffering from decision fatigue, they opted for the default choice—which, in the case of parole hearings, is to deny parole.

A similar phenomenon occurs at the polls. When voters have to sift through local issues before actually casting their votes, they show greater tendency to abstain or rely on decision shortcuts, like voting for the status quo or the first-listed candidate. That explains why so many people instinctively vote "down ballot" based on party lines without knowing the candidates' records, positions, or possibly even their names. A straight vote may be the result of ideological or party loyalty. But it's also blissfully decision-free.

For feedforward to work, it has to stick to simplicity. While it's tempting to try to fix all the wrongs we find in others, going after everything means getting little to nothing in return. It's neither helpful nor productive to pile on feedback that becomes too burdensome the moment it is delivered. Feedforward that is Particular rescues people from information overload and helps them focus their decision-making energy on one choice at a time. It's how Kobe Bryant energized his protégés and why the parole board fatigued. With feedforward, it's not just what we say but also how much of it we say at once.

Fast Fix: Feedforward Is **Particular**   REPAIR

1. Too much feedback leads to information overload and poor decision making.
2. Dial down feedback by focusing on only one issue at a time.
3. Keep it simple—clear goals, hard limits, and well-defined means. People only adopt what they think they can adapt.

4. AUTHENTIC

Time for a thought experiment: Carson and Jainie work for the same company and are due for performance reviews. They're both midcareer, with about ten years of experience under their belts. Scheduled to meet with the line manager, Carson and Jainie get their reviews on the same day, but with completely different results.

Carson's review is brutal. His manager scolds him for filing reports with grammatical errors, failing to show up on time for meetings, and demonstrating rude and boorish behavior around the office. At the end, he's asked to sign an action plan intended to address these concerns. Jainie's review is the total opposite. She's congratulated for being careful and exacting in her work, always being punctual, and treating her colleagues cheerfully and with respect. Her supervisor praises her work and urges her to keep it up. Jainie leaves feeling that she's on the right track.

The feedback Carson receives is unequivocally negative. The feedback Jainie receives is unquestionably upbeat.

So, who's better off?

Actually, it's a no-brainer.

Carson.

If you guessed wrong, you're in good company. Most of us assume that positive feedback drives positive outcomes. We've come to accept, almost reflexively, that performance is proportional to praise, such that if we want lots of one, we have to deliver more of the other. (We'll expose the flaws of that assumption in chapter 6.) Getting a review like Jainie's is great for our egos, but not necessarily good for our long-term professional growth. If the purpose of reviews is improvement—and not simply affirmation—then it turns out that Carson, dinged up by bad news, comes out way ahead.

It's for reasons like this that one of the most critical—and probably hardest—elements of feedforward to master is how to make it authentic. Authentic feedback doesn't pull any punches. It delivers a no-nonsense, radically honest view of performance, even when the information is negative in nature. To help others look toward future possibilities and not simply dwell on past events, we must present the most genuine, unfiltered, and frank picture that we can—even if it's not pretty and might cause others to get upset.

Most people will tell you they're not afraid of giving authentic feedback, just *negative* feedback. Some worry about creating conflict and hard feelings. Others fear that it will cause a drop-off in the employee's performance. So they sugarcoat it, disguise it with colorful euphemisms, or just plain avoid it altogether, all in the name of not rocking the boat. Aside from fudging up the future with half-truths, keeping negative feedback from employees when it's warranted is wrong for another reason.

They may actually want to hear it.

There is new evidence to support what some might consider counterintuitive—namely, that negative feedback does more, not less, to enhance performance on the job. Just how far that goes depends on a number of factors, like a person's age, past work experience, and mastery of the field, but management experts have detected strong signs that negative feedback (or corrective feedback, as some call it) can push performance in ways that praise and reinforcement cannot.

In a survey conducted by leadership firm Zenger Folkman, nearly one thousand employees supported the idea of receiving negative feedback at work. By roughly a three-to-one margin, they indicated that getting suggestions for improvement and being alerted to mistakes did more to improve their performance than positive feedback, which is usually expressed as praise or reinforcement. When asked to name something that could help their careers, fully 72 percent said they thought their performance would improve if their managers would provide corrective feedback. In other words, they wanted just one thing: authenticity.

A lot of that has to do with experience. Researchers found that people who consider themselves experts on a subject are drawn to negative feedback, while those who see themselves as novices tend to seek positive responses. In one experiment, students in beginning-level French classes and advanced-level French literature classes were asked what kind of instructor they'd like to have. If it were up to them, would they want a teacher who lavished praise and highlighted their strengths, or an instructor who routinely corrected their mistakes and offered critiques?

Students who had just started to learn the language wanted positive feedback and opted for the supportive teacher, while students with more experience taking French chose the critical teacher. Seeing themselves as experts, they were more interested in hearing about what they did wrong and how to correct it than being told that they were *excellente*.

The same trends showed up when researchers looked at the billion-dollar nail-care industry. Women who identified as "experts" claimed to use multiple nail-care products, visit beauty parlors several times a month, and regularly pay for manicures. Not only did they seek more negative feedback about their habits—like whether they chose the wrong shade of red or should skip the nail extensions—but they were also more likely to act on negative feedback by paying more for manicures or changing beauty parlors.

While the feedback divide between experts and novices may come down to confidence—people who are just starting out need more reassurance than those who've earned their chops—researchers actually detected another factor at work: motivation.

It turned out that experts and novices were moved by different impulses. Novices wanted to develop a sense of "commitment"—whether others found their work goals valuable. For them, getting positive feedback helped them identify which future steps to take. With experts, who already had a pretty good sense of direction, the goal of feedback was "progress"—knowing whether they were making strides in their work. In this regard, negative feedback was much more helpful to them in eliminating drags on their productivity.

So while novices seek positive feedback because it makes them feel good, experts prefer negative feedback because it helps them work better. But researchers are quick to caution that negative feedback only works if people find it constructive and nonthreatening. So as long as it isn't perceived as a put-down, negative feedback can enact more change than positive feedback. Its power lies in its authenticity.

Don't think you can shake the stigma of giving negative feedback? Then consider the pitfalls of going overly positive. At some point in your life, you've probably been served a "praise sandwich"—a slice of negative feedback stuffed between two positive comments. Teachers are notorious for cooking these up at parent conferences. "Mrs. Jones, your son Johnny has such incredible energy! Sometimes it gets the better of him and he becomes quite disruptive in class. But when he settles down, his work is just first rate!"

Translation: Johnny is struggling with a behavior problem. He's disruptive. Maybe even annoying. His outbursts interfere with the learning of others and possibly his own. But what does Mrs. Jones hear? *My son has such incredible energy! His work is just first rate!* She's too busy chewing on the ends of the sandwich to pay attention to what's tucked inside. And memory research tends to back this up as well, showing that people tend to remember the first and last items in a sequence but not what falls in between.

Instead of dishing out praise sandwiches, managers and teachers should order up a "feedback wrap": layers of authentic feedback wrapped up in a single serving. Jurgen Appelo, an executive coach, says that feedback wraps succeed where praise sandwiches do not. They're designed to bundle critical information for the receiver and communicate problems in their entirety. He lists five key ingredients:

1. CONTEXT: What's the problem?
2. OBSERVATIONS: What has happened?
3. EMOTIONS: What does this make you feel?
4. VALUE: What do you want to happen?
5. SUGGEST: Is there something I can do to make this happen?

The feedback wrap is honest and direct. There are no artificial distinctions between positive and negative comments, just an honest presentation of the facts. The tone is respectful and timely, and it shows that the person giving feedback is paying attention. But most important, feedback wraps capture feedforward at its Authentic best: Rather than chastise people about their past actions, they point them toward their future potential—not where they've been, but where they're going from here.

Fast Fix: Feedforward Is **Authentic**   REPAIR

1. Novices like positive feedback because it makes them feel good, while experts prefer negative feedback because it helps them work better.
2. Be sure your feedback is constructive, or else it may be perceived as a threat.
3. Beware the perils of being overly positive. Ditch "praise sandwiches" in favor of "feedback wraps."

5. IMPACT

The Cleveland Clinic had a problem. Regarded as one of the best health-care centers in the world, it is also one of the largest. Its main hospital, just east of downtown Cleveland, is a sprawling, fourteen-hundred-bed facility. It operates eighteen full-service family health centers across northeastern Ohio; a tertiary-care hospital in Weston, Florida; a brain treatment center in Las Vegas; a rehab and wellness facility in Toronto; and a digital facility in Abu Dhabi complete with a high-fidelity simulation center. In 2015, Cleveland Clinic employed nearly 50,000 employees, received over 6 million patient visits, admitted more than 160,000 acute cases, and had an operating revenue of $7.2 billion—more than Allergan, one of the world's largest makers of medical devices. It has ranked number one in the world for cardiac care since 1995.

But sometime in 2008, there were signs of trouble. Not with patient treatment—that was still world-class—but with the way patients experienced that care. If you've ever had the misfortune of being hospitalized, you may recall getting a survey by mail or phone anywhere from forty-eight hours to six weeks after discharge. It's called the Hospital Consumer Assessment of Healthcare Providers and Systems—HCAHPS for short.

HCAHPS is a federally mandated survey of patients' perspectives of hospital care. It contains eighteen core questions about critical aspects of patients' hospital experiences: communication with nurses and doctors, the responsiveness of hospital staff, the cleanliness and quietness of the hospital environment, pain management, communication about medicines, discharge information, and whether patients would recommend the hospital.

Starting that year, the Centers for Medicare & Medicaid Services (CMS), the federal agency that oversees the two largest government health-care programs, began making the survey scores publicly available online. Beyond releasing comparative data on the quality of care, CMS also fired a salvo: Starting in 2013, roughly $1 billion in Medicare payments to hospitals would be contingent on performance in these areas, and the amount at stake would double by 2017.

These new revelations shouldn't have been a problem for the Clinic, but they were. The year the CMS scores went public, its overall rating was just average, and its performance in some areas was borderline awful. It ranked in the bottom 4 percent for staff responsiveness and room cleanliness, 5 percent for whether the area near a patient's room was quiet at night, 14 percent for doctors' communication skills, and 16 percent for nurses' communication skills. The hospital known for curing everything from hemophilia to hernias had been diagnosed with a chronic ailment of its own: negative patient feedback.

But remember, this is the Cleveland Clinic. Nine of its highly regarded programs ranked among the top five specialties in *U.S. News and World Report*'s 2016 "Best Hospitals" issue, and four departments—heart, urology, gastroenterology, and kidney disorders—placed among the top two. Overall, it was named the second-best hospital in the United States, behind only the Mayo Clinic. So long as patients were getting top-notch medical care, the hospital's senior medical and executive team might have looked the other way.

Except they didn't. Determined to change course and deliver exceptional patient care, the Cleveland Clinic embarked on a systematic overhaul of its operational and caregiving practices. It created an Office of Patient Experience (OPE), a $9.2 million, 112-member "voice of the patient" enterprise that is responsible for conducting and analyzing patient surveys, tending to patients' complaints, training hospital employees, and working with hospital units to identify and fix problems.

Some of those problems were procedural. Until 2010, the clinic didn't mandate hourly rounding on patients; some units did it, others did not. But when the OPE discovered a correlation between higher patient-experience scores and hourly rounds, it launched a pilot program in the heart and vascular unit, the hospital's crown jewel, to see whether the solution had scale.

For a period of ninety days, the nurses or nursing assistants on designated floors were required to see patients every hour and ask them five questions: *Do you need anything? Do you have any pain? Do you need to be repositioned? Do you need your personal belongings moved closer to you? Do you need to go to the bathroom?* Notes were kept and meticulously tracked. In all, about four thousand patients participated in the trial, and the units that regularly kept up with the rounds placed among the top 10 percent of nursing-related questions in the CMS survey the next year.

Other issues were functional: Teams of caregivers were not communicating with one another. Doctors didn't consult with nurses. Social workers and case managers didn't work together to establish discharge plans. Hospital floors with as many as three separate specialties and staffs operated in silos.

To reestablish better lines of communication, the OPE recommended "weekly huddles" consisting of a floor nurse manager; an assistant nurse manager; a physician from the specialty that had the most patients on the floor; the housekeeping services supervisor; a social worker; and the case manager responsible for discharge, insurance, and at-home needs. They would discuss patient complaints, try to address their concerns, and streamline the process of communication among multiple caregivers. The weekly huddles helped improve CMS scores in less than a month.

Three years later, when CMS released its scores for 2011, the Cleveland Clinic had been given a clean bill of health. Based on the actionable changes it made to improve patient experience, its overall ranking in the survey of patient satisfaction jumped from about average to among the top 8 percent of the roughly forty-six hundred hospitals included. The Clinic's "Patients First" mantra has been emulated by health-care providers all around the world, eager to learn how even one of the world's greatest hospitals managed to reinvent itself.

There's a fundamental truth behind the turnaround, and it's that feedback is only fruitful when it makes an Impact. While this part comes toward the end of the REPAIR plan, it is arguably one of the most important. We can make our feedback more particular. We can adjust our questions to expand creative possibilities. We can even ensure that our feedback regenerates talent and stays authentic. But if our feedback doesn't translate into impact, then all we're doing is a lot of talking, because—as the old saying goes—actions speak louder than words.

Obviously, anyone who gives feedback is hoping that it will yield results. That's the point, right? But if problems of performance or personality could be solved just by *talking* about them, then feedback would put people on offense, not defense. They'd take our suggestions and start to run with them. Instead, a great deal of feedback quickly turns to pushback—denial, resistance, sometimes even anger. Why does that happen? Is it because people are unwilling to listen to feedback? Unable to learn from it? Or, perhaps, it is something else entirely: They are unsure of how to *live with it*—how to make the feedback a recognizable part of their lives.

The scary part of feedback is knowing what to do with it next. For many people, it's like getting prescription medication without instructions for use. They're willing to swallow the pills; they just need to know how. Acting on feedback is no different. In the end, the hang-up isn't compliance. It's transfer.

Transfer is the surefire sign of feedforward that makes an Impact. It's more than just a roadmap or a blueprint. It's a *plan*. Transfer is the deliberate process of taking vague concepts and turning them into hard commitments. Basically, it's how words become deeds, ideas become strategies, and visions become realities. And for any of that to happen, there can't just be a broad end goal—there has to be series of short-term steps shaping the path. Dan and Chip Heath, in their wonderful book *Switch*, call this "shrinking the change." Instead of setting up milestones, we should be laying down pebbles—smaller steps that pave the way for bigger strides.

When feedback fails to produce real results or noticeable improvement, the first question we ought to ask is whether it suffered from a transfer problem. It is neither fair nor reasonable to expect someone to change a long-standing practice or personality trait on the basis of a single directive—or even a few conversations. Transfer occurs when there's a clear destination in sight, with frequent stops along the way. Each stop is defined, aligned, and primed around the needs of the person and the goals of the process. But until we give others the sense that they're headed somewhere, feedback goes nowhere. It ends up producing short-term frustration, not long-term solutions.

So how do you give people the feeling that they're in motion? By asking them to lead the charge.

Bruce Joyce and Beverly Showers have spent the better part of thirty years exploring the concept of transfer and why some practitioners turn knowledge into action while others do not. Take an area where transfer is critical: the classroom. There's no denying the cumulative impact of teacher effectiveness on student learning. And while great teachers certainly owe a good deal of their success to natural talent, great teaching is the product of excruciatingly hard work, long practice, and ongoing learning. But what Joyce and Showers found is that even exceptional teachers do not automatically transfer knowledge to practice. In fact, when learning remains a passive and theoretical exercise, the transfer rate is *exactly zero*. Take a look:

	Knowledge	Skill	Transfer
Theory	10%	5%	0%
Demonstration	30%	20%	0%
Practice	60%	60%	5%
Coaching	95%	95%	95%

Alternatively, when teachers became more actively involved in their own learning through hands-on practice and coaching, their transfer rates skyrocket. Coaching—with its mirror-holding emphasis on self-discovery, as we saw earlier—is how feedback breaks down big goals into small steps and ultimately makes an Impact. Teachers who are actively coached are more likely to try to retain new strategies and skills, explain new models of teaching to their students so they understand their purpose, and exhibit clearer understandings of when and how to use certain techniques. They learn how to master the art of transfer, one move at a time.

It's not hard to imagine a similar dynamic playing out in families as well. Parents who want their kids to follow through on feedback shouldn't resort to demanding, bribing, or other losing propositions. To get to transfer, they should set a big goal—say, getting organized—and invite kids to lay down their own pebble path for short-term success.

Older kids can probably come up with action steps on their own: Put the homework in the folder. Check the dining room table for missing textbooks. Pack a gym bag the night before. Write a reminder on the refrigerator whiteboard. Younger kids may need more guidance in forming the sequence but can still have a strong voice in setting the steps. It doesn't matter what the target is or where it's happening. The best way to shrink the change is to let others lead the charge.

Fast Fix: Feedforward Makes an **Impact**   REPAIR

1. It's not an unwillingness to comply but an inability to transfer that keeps people from making progress.

2. When leading others to act, start with a big end goal ("milestones") and line the path with smaller steps ("pebbles").

3. People can't take action unless they are active. Let them suggest their own ideas for getting things done.

---

6. REFINES

Thermostats are humble things. They hang meekly on the wall, overshadowed by framed pictures and handled less often than their more prominent neighbor, the light switch. They don't command the attention or interest of, say, a home security system, and they're not much to look at, either. Earlier versions resembled misplaced doorknobs, and more recent attempts, like the clunky rectangular panel with the flip-top lid, aren't exactly a visual upgrade. Even as home design has become sleeker and more technologically advanced, thermostats have stayed mostly the same. People find them, well, boring.

Not Tony Fadell and Matt Rogers. The former Apple duo—Fadell created the iPod, and Rogers led software development for the iPhone—decided they wanted to reprogram the thermostat's image for good. Instead of a mechanical lump that needed to be adjusted manually throughout the day, Fadell and Rogers imagined a device that was intelligent enough to learn and anticipate its owners' preferences. So in 2011, with only ten employees, no investor cash, and a two-car garage in Palo Alto, they set out to build the world's first smart thermostat.

Eighteen months later, the Nest Learning Thermostat arrived: a striking stainless-steel-ringed disc with a circular display featuring hardware components that were closer to those of an iPhone than a thermostat. Its built-in artificial intelligence noted owners' preferred settings, then adjusted temperatures on its own based on the time of day and whether people were around. It even put itself into energy-save mode when necessary. Nest estimates that its $250 product has kept owners from using 225 million kilowatt hours of energy, saving them around $29 million at average U.S. prices.

For such an unheralded product, the market potential is huge. More than ten million thermostats are sold in the United States every year, and thermostats control about 50 percent of the energy burned in the home—somewhere in the annual range of $2,200. Overall, the home energy sector accounts for 10 percent of total energy consumption nationwide, which explains in part why Google (now Alphabet) snatched up Nest in 2014 for a cool $3.2 billion. In the acquisition, Nest's founders retained creative control, which seemed rather fitting given their unusual approach to building products: The only thing more remarkable about Nest's futuristic thermostat was the innovative way it was developed.

Instead of simply turning the project over to engineers, which is what you might expect when dealing with a hardware problem, Nest compiled a diverse team of user-experience experts, product managers, software developers, algorithm analysts, and marketing executives—none of whom had ever tried to hack the HVAC business before. To industry watchers, it seemed like a promotional stunt. What could a marketing person possibly have to say about the design and operation of a thermostat?

But with its unorthodox approach, Nest was trying to generate something known in management circles as "creative abrasion," or the innovation that is sparked when opposing views converge.

Imagine you're the Nest engineer sitting across the table from a marketing guy who probably flunked high school physics. He may not know much about alternating currents or rechargeable batteries, but he keenly understands how to wrap those technical elements into a product vision that people will love—and are willing to pay for. What at first seemed headed for a collision course turned out to be an on ramp for faster ideation and decision making. Creative abrasion helped the team link all stages of product development, from hardware to advertising, rather than address them in isolation.

Without berating or bemoaning, the Nest team worked through the abrasion by avoiding the rough patches of conflict. They recognized one another as knowledge sources. They listened to each other's criticism, even if it meant swallowing personal pride. And they avoided giving direct orders, even if a senior member of the team could rightfully call rank. In the end, all their unique and occasionally clashing views—some coming from those with no apparent knowledge of the engineering problem at hand—collapsed into a single, albeit unusual, vision that gave rise to a thermostat so improbable, so unrecognizable, it just might change the way people live.

And it did.

By taking the commanding tone out of feedback and replacing it with something more collaborative, the Nest team showed the persuasive power of feedforward that Refines group dynamics. When people give feedback, they have a tendency to use the medium as a way to flex authority and control—to coerce instead of coach, and to impose their perspective and ideas on others. That, in turn, creates a two-tier feedback dynamic, with the feedback giver on top. The message that trickles down to the receiver is one-sided, giver-focused, and prescriptive in nature. In these feedback scenarios, there's not much for the receiver to do other than acquiesce.

But with its Refines approach, feedforward opens up more of a dialogue about what should come next. The giver sets the near-term goals and then slides over to make room for the receiver to fill the open space. Unlike traditional feedback, which thrives on hierarchy and power, feedforward creates progress through partnership and makes people feel like they're co-creators in the development process—which, by its very nature, can lead to some unexpected breakthroughs along the way.

Case in point: The first Nest devices to ship were an engineering wonder—so smart, in fact, that they outmaneuvered their owners by greedily lowering temperatures in the winter and raising them in the summer when they learned people weren't around. Customers balked, protesting that their thermostat was forcing them to adopt conditions they didn't want. And if the thermostat continued to dominate their lifestyle habits, they didn't want *it*, either.

So the marketing team introduced a clever hook. When homeowners selected a temperature-saving level, they were rewarded for their eco-friendliness with a digital badge: an endearing-looking green leaf that appears just beneath the temperature. It was a small gesture, but it went over beautifully with consumers, who vied to add to their running leaf count each month based on the interactions they had with their thermostat. Instead of telling customers how to conserve energy, Nest shrewdly got them to do it themselves.

That was no accident. The first-generation model, produced by engineers, used artificial intelligence to save people money. But it was the later version—informed by marketers—that figured out how to leverage human nature by tapping into the need for recognition and control. If Nest didn't encourage these views to collide, it would have ended up making the world's smartest thermostat that consumers didn't want.

Of course, just because feedforward Refines group dynamics doesn't mean it will always lead to consensus. All those converging opinions can, of course, just as easily combust, which is why some leaders resort to "safe" teams made up of people who come from the same backgrounds, draw from the same experiences, and even hail from the same units or disciplines. Their sameness may hold them together, but when it comes to creating new ideas, challenging old assumptions, or testing different practices, it may very well keep them apart.

Learning how to align teams with feedforward is something that's explored more broadly in chapter 5, but the following tips—courtesy of the people who coined "creative abrasion" nearly two decades ago—can help leaders put some finishing touches on their refining fix:

- *Know the styles of the team.* It's essential that team leaders know the makeup of their team members. Pairing night owls with early risers can lead to some obvious tempo issues. Same goes for work style. You don't want to mix procrastinators and planners. Some people need frequent check-ins; others may only want occasional updates. Finding the right team dynamics takes a fair amount of time and tuning, but the smooth finish is worth it. When styles clash, ideas don't collide.

- *Keep project goals at the forefront.* Even fearless leadership has to come down to earth and eventually push for "convergent thinking"—the building of consensus around a single goal and plan of action. Too much deliberation clogs up the productivity pipeline. Options must be reduced. Resolutions must be made. One way leaders can proactively steer others from debating to deciding is by establishing specific parameters and time lines from the start. The same goes for classroom collaboration and project-based learning. Ultimately, there must be rules for how the work gets done and an end in sight. Just like in basketball, if you hold on to the ball too long, you run out the clock.

- *Create clear guidelines for how teams will work.* Remember, it's called *abrasion* for a reason. For teams trying to fix dynamics by refining them, they need a protocol for handling conflict if it ensues. For starters, there are several changes they can make off the bat: State expectations about how members speak to one another from the outset—no personal attacks, no dismissive body language, no snarky side comments. Support positions with facts, not feelings. Raise objections with a rationale. Don't shut down an idea unless you're prepared to open up a new one in its place. As long as everyone accepts that pushback isn't personal, clarity beats agreement, hands down.

And, of course, no team can flourish without exceptional support from leaders and teachers who, in the view of Marcus Buckingham, understand people's strengths, move them into positions and rearrange work to leverage these strengths, and coach them to build on these strengths. Not only do these tactics increase professional capacity and performance, but they also give people the comfort of knowing that someone is standing by their side, which can have a dramatic effect on the way they perceive their work and surroundings.

Turns out, there's a scientific basis for it, too. Researchers found that when participants had to estimate the slope of a hill from its base to its top, they guessed it to be less steep if they were joined by a friend. The same held true of participants who merely *thought* of a supportive friend while performing an imagery task—they saw the hill as less steep compared to those who thought of either a neutral person or a disliked person. Partnership, which lies at the heart of feedforward that Refines, changes the way we see things, often for the better.

Benjamin Franklin is famously reported to have said the same: "Tell me and I forget. Teach me and I may remember. Involve me and I learn." It's possible to create major performance turnarounds—just ask the doctors at the Cleveland Clinic—but until we get others involved in the process of setting, staging, and scaffolding goals, feedback will probably just lead to more talk, not transfer. When feedback sticks to the future and starts giving people a say in how it looks, it delivers a much-needed boost in performance and potential. The REPAIR plan creates the fix, but it's the impact of feedforward on everyday life—the way others work, learn, and lead—that helps them substantially upgrade their lives. The next section looks at how.

Fast Fix: Feedforward **Refines** Group Dynamics

1. Flatter organizations don't just do away with hierarchies. They make people feel like they're partners in their own development process.

2. Establish working conditions so that divergent thinking eventually turns into convergent thinking.

3. With the right support, creative abrasion can lead to idea breakthroughs, not breakdowns.

II

THE UPGRADE

3

Creativity

From the outside, the Rama School looks pretty ordinary. The two-story yellow stucco building sits on a leafy corner in Israel's Ramat HaSharon neighborhood, located along the country's central coastal strip, just minutes from the glistening tech hub of Tel Aviv. The grounds are sparse, mostly bare except for a few lonely slides and wooden seesaws scattered along the perimeter. A dusty, rectangular field serves as the school's playground and impromptu soccer arena, enclosed by wrought iron fences with white paint that has weathered time and an assortment of wildly thrown balls.

Compared to American schools, the classrooms here are relatively small, but still spacious enough to fit about a dozen desks, chairs, and a few wall-length folding tables. By design, there is a conspicuous lack of technology—none of the interactive whiteboards, laptop carts, or mounted projectors you might expect to find in schools nowadays. The walls show signs of wear, but colorful displays of student work disguise most of it.

There's not a whole lot of filing or cabinet space, so most of the consumables are tucked away in portable crates and bins. Aside from the usual stash of art supplies, you might also discover a small collection of gardening spades, woodworking tools, and metal sifters. In the science lab, rows of graduated cylinders and droppers sit behind glass-paneled units that reflect the salty-blue tones of the walls. Blue is by far the most popular color—from window shades and curtains to door paint, everything feels like the nearby Mediterranean, just calmer. Most of the time, the building is quiet. Actually, it's usually empty, and with good reason. Students only show up here one day a week.

That's right, *one day.*

Rama is home to one of Israel's fifty-five enrichment programs for gifted and talented children in third to eighth grade. Operated jointly by the Ministry of Education and the local municipality, Rama offers a mix of practicums and interdisciplinary classes taught by specialists in the sciences, arts, and humanities. Students who score in the top tier on a national exam are eligible to enter the program at Rama one day a week instead of taking their usual spots at the public schools in and around Ramat HaSharon, an arid city with a population of roughly fifty thousand.

The goal of the program is to deepen students' learning by radically re-designing the learning experience. Over the course of a six-hour day, nearly one hundred students cycle through three ninety-minute lessons that look and function more like design labs. Unlike the public schools, which employ traditional block scheduling based on a child's age and grade, Rama flexibly groups its students by their learning interests, allowing preteens to choose class electives like they're college freshmen.

The school does not follow strict curricular mandates, impose rigid teaching standards, or test students to death. It doesn't have to. With a selectively talented population, Rama can loosen the constraints of a one-size curriculum and stake its pedagogy on critical thinking and collaboration, giving high-achieving students a chance to go deeper and wider all at once.

Walking into class, you get the sense that there's not a whole lot of formality—or sitting, for that matter. Students prefer to huddle in small groups, occasionally migrating to different corners of the room. Some work at long, skinny desks; others pace along the perimeter. The learning tempo is brisk but casual, which suits the fifteen or so students per class just fine. That same air of playfulness spills out into the narrow hallways, which are crammed with colorful backpacks hanging from hooks that resemble miniature foosball players.

But beneath its typical facade, Rama is breaking the molds of traditional education. Its unusual class lineup includes whimsical topics like "The Science of Juggling" and "Flight through Space." In a single day, students can join an archeology dig, learn puppeteering, deconstruct mathematical proofs, and design an animated feature film. Around here, learning happens mostly by doing, often in surprisingly unconventional ways.

That's because nearly all the educators at Rama aren't professionally trained teachers. In fact, almost none of them have formally studied education or received teaching certifications. The faculty includes a marine biologist, an architect, an animation director, a NASA researcher, and even a competitive chess player. By turns, each of them casts a spell of curiosity and wonder that gets students thinking and behaving differently. They unlock a creative force that resides in every child, if only for a day. But as one teacher at Rama has discovered, the secret isn't how they teach.

It's what they say.

THE CREATIVITY CONUNDRUM

By his own admission, Elad Segev knows more about chemistry than creativity. Actually, he knows a lot more about chemistry than most people. Segev holds a PhD in theoretical chemical physics and has completed postdoctoral work in applied mathematics at Israel's prestigious Weizmann Institute of Science. His academic pedigree earned him a spot on a research and development team at a leading pharmaceutical company exploring treatments for cystic fibrosis. With a profile like his, the last place you'd expect to find Segev is sitting behind a desk planning lessons for preteens.

But that's exactly where he ended up. During a round of contract talks with his lab, Segev made an unusual request: He wanted to take a one-day leave each week to teach at a local school, something he'd been doing since his college days. "I saw it as an opportunity to give back to the community, but my boss thought I was crazy," he recalled. "He couldn't understand what an R&D guy was doing in a classroom with young kids." His company granted the time off, and Segev joined a new school for gifted and talented students opening up in his neighborhood. It was Rama.

After several months of running double duty, Segev started to feel like his wings had been clipped. An internal reorganization at the lab brought new research heads and management styles. "My environment was the same, but people talked to me differently." The changes put a freeze on his creativity. "I used to come up with new angles in our research each week. Suddenly, it just stopped," he said. Segev knew something had knocked him off track but couldn't quite place it. The way his superiors spoke to him seemed to curtail his creativity. The effects were real, but not quite discernable.

Burdened by stress at the lab, he returned to Rama each week hypermindful of the way he communicated with students. "After a lesson, I'd be thinking about my interactions for days," he said. *Were my instructions too simple? What kind of responses did students receive from me?* Segev found himself replaying these classroom scenes in his mind, all the while thinking of his own feedback drama at work.

He eventually realized that the narrowness of his assignments had created a talent trap. Conditioned by years of "skill and drill" education, the brainy students at Rama had come to treat learning like a game of whack-a-mole, swatting down easy prompts just as quickly as they appeared. When one simple task popped up, students raced to knock it down. Then another. And another. If you quickly master a skill, doing the drill isn't much of a challenge. For them, going to school felt like living inside a giant arcade game—lots of repetition and mindless motion, just without the game tokens and chintzy prizes.

A typical day in the public schools meant a never-ending run of check-the-box assignments and rote exercises. These kids quickly conquered low-level targets the way gamers advance through rounds of *Super Mario Brothers*. After a while, school became an utterly predictable and passionless experience. They had figured out how to cross the goal line without running up tempo or breaking a sweat. It's hard to blame them. Why bother to stretch when you can just cruise?

"I had this feeling that students were gaming the system," explained Segev. "They knew exactly what I wanted from them and did just that. Nothing more. I wanted them to produce better work, more dynamic work, but it wasn't there." For all their technical smarts, the students seemed to lack a curious spirit, the will to tinker and wonder. They appeared to be more preoccupied with completing assigned tasks than generating imaginative ideas. They had busied themselves out of creativity.

And then it struck. Segev realized that while creativity can't be conditioned, it can thrive in the right *conditions*. To reach full strength, creativity requires a certain amount of freedom—just enough flexibility, choice, and space to sprout. Unlike goods and services, creativity can't be ordered on demand. It evolves slowly, bubbling up in small batches—some here, a little there—until it finally overtakes whatever came before. But when the limits are too tight, people hold back. They won't test boundaries that don't seem movable.

Now it all clicked. Segev's productivity drop-off at the lab and the middling efforts of Rama students in class were casualties of the same cause: too much control, not enough choice. Without the freedom to think, wonder, and explore, neither Segev nor his students could break through. They were stuck beneath the heavy lid of other people's prescriptions—the outcomes that *they* wanted. Bound tightly by an outside will, creativity hadn't vanished. It just lacked room to grow.

Helping it reemerge would take more than just changing the messenger. To really unleash the kind of creativity that Segev and his students craved, there had to be a change in the message itself—to develop something closer to people's creative cores. Being authoritarian and telling others what to do silences the quiet potential that resides inside every person—the parts of themselves that are "naturally" savvy and smart. That could include areas of technical skill, like writing code or editing a draft; tactical smarts, like planning and executing a project; and transformational strengths, like knowing intuitively how to move others to action.

This is where feedforward can make a difference. Remember "creative abrasion" from back in chapter 2? Not only is it a key element of feedforward that Refines, but it is also the driving force behind how people learn and retain information. Throwing different elements together turns people into active partners and planners in the feedback process. When it comes to doing better and more creative work, people already have the tools. What they need is the space to use them the way they know best.

So we have a choice: rely on traditional feedback and blanket people with what *we* know, or resort to feedforward and help people uncover what *they* know. The consequences of that choice are greater than we think. It amounts to the difference between gazing through a window and looking at a mirror. When two people gaze through a window, they study the same scene but may reach completely different conclusions. Their views might end up being so dissimilar, so irreconcilable, they might as well be gazing into a kaleidoscope. If they happen to be equals—coworkers, perhaps, or good friends—then it's possible for them to find consensus, iron out any differences, and meld their opposing renditions into a shared view. In a relationship of equality, two can become one.

But with traditional feedback, the relationship is never about equality—it's about power. One leads, the other follows. One talks, the other listens. This means that only one view can prevail—and because power resides with the feedback giver, the receiver's view gets dimmed completely. It doesn't matter what the receiver sees—only how the giver sees him or her. Feedback that comes from window gazing almost always puts the receiver at a disadvantage.

Something entirely different happens when we trade windows for mirrors. When one person holds up a mirror for someone else to stare into, there's only one view—the reflection that stares back at the one who's looking. And that's the only view that counts, of course, since all the other person can see is the mirror's opaque backside. This time, it's the feedback receiver, not the giver, who has the superior perspective, since he sees the one person he knows best: himself. Mirror holding is how we help others discover the creative talent that's waiting to be released.

That kind of self-revelation isn't likely to happen under the authoritarian wing of traditional feedback. With its dead-end message and restrictive tone, traditional feedback depletes our creative capital. We don't feel compelled to push the limits of our imagination or push back against the boundaries of conventional thinking. Great ideas must cross a threshold if they're ever going to make it into the world. Window gazing sees only obstacles. Mirror holding reveals hidden opportunities.

WHAT WAFERS TELL US ABOUT CREATIVITY

So if traditional feedback operates like a straitjacket, how do people ever break loose? The answer may depend on how we choose to deliver that feedback. If feedback is closed, imposed, and rear-facing, then we should expect people to end up in knots. But if our message is open, autonomous, and future-leaning, can they find some room to maneuver around? The scientist in Segev wanted to find out.

On a sunny autumn morning, he stopped at a local convenience store on his way into Rama and picked up several dozen vanilla wafers, two big tubes of chocolate frosting, and a few containers of rainbow-colored sprinkles. Judging by the contents of his shopping cart, you'd think he was planning a party, not a learning exercise. He tucked the goods inside his briefcase, right on top of the modeling clay he had secretly swiped from his children's art cabinet the night before. His audience: three different groups of seventh through ninth graders at Rama (In Israel, high school begins in tenth grade.)

When the first round of middle schoolers arrived at 8:15 a.m., Segev greeted them with a big smile and a carefully worded prompt, scrawled in big block letters on the white board: *Spread chocolate frosting on a wafer. Then create a structure that will prevent sprinkles from sticking to it.* With some fanfare, Segev pretended to launch an aerial assault by rattling sealed containers of multicolored sprinkles over plates full of chocolatey targets. To defend their helpless treats, students could only rely on a few designated materials, including modeling clay, a box of matches, and some craft sticks. Game on.

Segev repeated the instructions out loud and made sure that every student understood the task's limitations. *Create a structure. Use only preapproved materials.* Segev didn't tack on a time limit, but once he gave the green light, most students completed their mission in just a matter of minutes. When they finished working, their "structures" looked awfully similar: a sheet of modeling clay resting atop some matches and craft sticks, with the wafers nestled safely below.

True to form, the group conquered the task quickly, efficiently, and without a whole lot of creativity. Based on the crude uniformity of their designs, it was clear that the students had visualized the simplest and most direct solution: *Make a protective roof.* The products from this first round confirmed Segev's earlier suspicions about feedback. Narrowly worded, restrictive instructions like "build a structure" had triggered a simplified, unimaginative response. Their wafer fortresses looked impenetrable but painfully plain.

The bell rang. After a short break, a second group of middle schoolers filed in, but this time Segev tweaked the assignment. Instead of imposing limits on his instructions, he motioned to the wafers and told his wide-eyed audience to simply prevent the sprinkles from landing on the frosted treats. No mention of available materials. No limitations of time. Segev didn't even specify that students should "build a structure," like he did with the students from the first round. The only requirement was to make the solution sprinkle-proof, which is exactly what they did—and in more ways than one.

Four students paired off and cupped their hands over the wafers like a bomb shelter. A few encased the wafers in protective armor made out of empty match boxes. Others flipped the wafers over, so that the frosted side faced the plate. And some really clever kids, sensing an opportunity, opted for a delicious alternative. They simply ate the wafers.

Segev recalls the mood in the room: "They were very joyous as they worked. Students laughed and worked together. They spoke to one another about their plans and teamed up to find solutions." During a debrief with students, Segev uncovered the reason behind their brain burst. Unencumbered by rote tasks or restrictive language, the students felt free to dream up creative possibilities. Segev didn't need to tell them how to plan or what to do. They figured that out on their own.

But the most revealing moment came during the final rotation. A third group of students arrived at Segev's classroom for last period. By now, many of them had heard about the edible activity and took their seats eager to dig in. But Segev had other plans. "I wanted to see how stress and competition influenced the creative process," he said, "and so this version had to be structured differently than the ones before."

Segev announced that two students would face off in a timed competition to see who could beat the wafer challenge. To add to the drama, he positioned the contestants at the same table with a makeshift divider between them. The rest of the class formed a large semicircle around the players to cheer them on and watch the clock. As students visibly tensed up, Segev described how the competition would be scored. Materials would be limited to the supplies on the table. Only one person would be declared the winner. There would be no consolation prize for the runner-up, no partial credit, and no points for simply trying.

What happened next was an exercise in futility.

Pressured by time and the clamoring crowd, neither student could mount much of a challenge. Each one hastily constructed a few simple designs, fumbled over his or her materials, and stared helplessly at the tray of wafers, which by now held the appeal of a plate of seaweed. The faster they tried to work, the sloppier they became. Their frustration was so painful to watch that Segev called off the contest. Their ill-formed products barely passed for a shelter.

Think about it. The samples from the three groups were nearly identical—same number of kids, same range of intelligence, same readiness for learning. The basic goal of the exercise—to prevent sprinkles from landing on a frosted wafer—remained unchanged from class to class. Students had access to the same materials, sat inside the same classroom, and received both written and verbal instructions. But for all their sameness, each group produced a different response, from simple to imaginative to all-out disaster.

One lesson, three outcomes. The subtle changes in Segev's communications proved to be a difference maker, the invisible cord that swung students toward success or failure, imagination or dullness, joy or frustration. His feedback quite literally changed their future outcomes. But to understand why, we need to trace the patterns of creativity all the way back to their source.

THE CREATIVE MIND

Like everything else about us, our creativity originates inside the soft, grayish-white enclaves of the human brain. Truth be told, we actually have two brains—or, to be exact, two regions of the mind that dictate how we perceive our world and interact with it. Scientifically speaking, these spaces are known as the brain's two hemispheres, which operate separately but in lockstep. Lodged on one side is our left brain (sometimes called the "digital" brain), which acts like a verbal locomotive. It helps us process information through sequential and analytical thinking, the kind of mental heavy lifting required for logic and calculation.

To do this, the left brain scans tiny pieces of information that cross our neural dashboard and forms them into a cohesive whole. When we read or write, our left brain rapidly fires neural signals to help us make sense out of millions of fragments—letters, words, figures, ideas, and the like. It also goes to work any time we try to recall a rote fact, like the capital of Texas (Austin) or the first secretary of the Treasury (Alexander Hamilton). In real time, the left brain pulls desired information from our memory warehouse and delivers it straight to our cognitive doorstep. It's kind of like Amazon for the mind.

Then there's the right brain, its visual counterpart. Instead of processing information through logic and sequence, the right brain (also called the "analog" brain) applies the filters of intuition and interpretation. When our eyes catch sight of an object, the right brain looks at the whole picture and then reconstitutes it. That regenerative ability—to snap a mental picture and then deconstruct it into disparate parts—puts the right brain in charge of our three-dimensional sense, artistic expression, and, as you might have guessed, our creativity.

Although the latest brain research would seem to indicate that we use both hemispheres of our brains nearly all the time, their functional difference shows up in critical ways. The left brain helps us think in words. The right brain lets us communicate through pictures. Left-brain activity computes facts. Right-brain activity visualizes features. The thinking we do with our left brain leads down a narrow path of linear processing and sequencing. The thinking we do with our right brain winds along the curves of our imagination.

Exactly where these cognitive detours will lead is anyone's guess, but if we want people to exercise their creativity, then we need to relax the process—literally. Joydeep Bhattacharya, a psychologist at Goldsmiths, University of London, has monitored brain activity to anticipate a stroke of creative insight up to eight seconds before it arrives. But that predictive power only applied to subjects whose brain scans showed a steady rhythm of alpha waves, a mysterious neural signal associated with calming sensations.

Alpha waves stream from the brain's right hemisphere, the zip code for creativity. Bhattacharya discovered that when people enjoyed higher levels of relaxation, their alpha wave output picked up, which prompted them to train their focus inward, toward the right brain's creative juices. By contrast, individuals who slipped into states of intense concentration tended to shift their attention away from the brain's creative command center and in the direction of the task at hand.

For someone who's crunching data or analyzing information, this outward shift is actually quite helpful. The degree of concentration required for these highly linear tasks is best routed through the brain's left hemisphere, which lights up anytime we become engrossed in logic and reason. That, in turn, helps produce a clear solution, an obvious lead. After all, the left brain is exceptionally adept at generating a series of logical, sequential connections—in other words, the fastest, most obvious answer to any given problem.

But the stress-producing act of deep concentration also sets us adrift, far away from the creative islets of our cognitive channels. The more intensely we study a problem, the duller our right brains become. That's not to say that the right hemisphere doesn't participate in problem solving at some level—the science shows it does—but it won't supercharge its creative capacities until the mind reaches a more relaxed state. "That's why so many insights happen during warm showers," Bhattacharya says. "For many people, it's the most relaxing part of their day."

Some highly celebrated breakthroughs in creativity seem to follow this script. Take 3M, the maker of consumer products like water purification systems, kitchen sponges, dental fillings, and, most famously, Scotch Tape. From its earliest years, 3M has encouraged its employees to take intermittent breaks during the workday. At any given hour, workers abandon their cubicles and roam the sprawling grounds at 3M headquarters, located just outside of St. Paul, Minnesota. If Thoreau worked in corporate America, this might be his Walden Pond.

But 3M doesn't just tolerate breaks. It also pushes distraction—the kind that leads to discovery. The company that brought us Post-it notes urges employees to devote 15 percent of their workday to speculative pursuits, a practice it internally calls "bootlegging." The thinking goes something like this: If creativity can't be commanded—just gently coaxed during moments of supreme calm—then the path to innovation leads through imagination. So if 3M wants its team to create the next big thing in consumer products, it isn't going to happen if its workers are moving to the rhythm of routine. They need a cognitive change of scenery.

Clipping a page from 3M's playbook, Google has rebooted the bootleg-ging strategy with its highly touted policy of "20 percent time." Employees can devote the equivalent of an entire workday to chasing ambitious projects and other moonshots. We'll never know for sure—Google doesn't talk about it—but it's likely that many of these efforts fizzled before making it to market. The dream ended up in a heap of disappointment. It turns out that some ideas aren't so hot once they leave our heads.

But for all the dead ends and rabbit holes, 20 percent time has produced some spectacular successes, like Gmail and AdSense, the profit engine that drives the company's eye-popping search revenue. Eager to imitate, just about every start-up in Silicon Valley now preaches the gospel of innovation and relaxation. They design work spaces that look like adult playrooms. But the ubiquitous foosball tables, game consoles, and plush lounge chairs aren't just about creating a good workplace vibe. They're also about building a bet-ter business—and a more creative workforce. And that's where feedforward proves to be a game changer.

THE STANDOFF

It's tantalizing to imagine what all of this might mean as we educate the work-force of the future. In the last fifteen years, we've produced two major pieces of school reform: the stiff (and, to some, punitive) performance standards of No Child Left Behind, which Congress retired in 2015, and the competitive, incentives-laden Race to the Top grant program. Each initiative took aim at academic underperformance, just from different sides. But regardless of whether legislation looked more like a stick or a carrot, the conversation stayed focused on standardization—getting districts and schools to bend themselves in the same direction, especially when it came to teaching and learning.

The problem with uniformity, as far as education goes, is that learning is rarely uniform. In a digital age of disruptive learning, students can choose how and when they study. They register new information at different rates and retain prior knowledge with varying results. From a delivery standpoint, more teachers than ever before accept the premise that students are "smart" in lots of different ways and thus provide multiple entry points for learning. As the landscape shifts, so do teacher mind-sets. They are becoming increasingly attuned to the things that make students different, not the same.

But tapping into that unique learning profile is a lot harder in practice. Designing the right size and path of education for a whole bunch of students requires long hours and deep patience. Managing a differentiated classroom requires agility and discipline, with teachers' roles wedged somewhere between symphony conductor and traffic cop. Hacking that is still only half the battle. Customization works well when students fall within a typical performance range but less so when their readiness flies all over the map. It's not every day that teachers get to engage students as selectively gifted or compliant as Elad Segev's wafer-eating troupe.

That's just the sobering view from the ground floor. The picture gets more complicated a few levels up, which is where teachers face the heavy managerial hand of central offices mandating lots of paperwork, documentation, and value-added evaluations designed to link teacher performance to student test scores. These measures are well intended, and the people who create them are well meaning. Yet none of these actions actually improves teaching. As a form of feedback, they are more or less ineffective—that is, more about control, less about improvement.

What we have then, in the parlance of management expert Clayton Christensen, is the educator's dilemma: teachers who may recognize the unique needs of learners but who must operate within a system driven by the uniform demands of curriculum. That tension, expressed in learning encounters every day, forces a standoff between coverage and quality. With coverage, the burning question is *"Did we get to it?"* With quality, the animating issue is *"Did they understand it?"* In this dynamic, you've got the teacher's need for progress pitted against the student's need for purpose.

Set up like a battleground, everyday interactions between teachers and students suffer, especially the feedback that's shared. Racing to teach content means that teachers don't spend as much time giving feedback on how students are learning and where they could be doing better. It's not that teachers dislike giving feedback. They're just moving too quickly to spend much time on it.

When coverage is king, instruction gets sucked toward the academic mid-range, which is where most of the action usually happens. In a typical class, odds are that about one-third of the students are hopelessly bored (already know it), confused (have no clue), or asleep (bored and confused). That lumps the other two-thirds somewhere in the middle, and now teaching has become a game of darts: You aim for the center, take your best shot, and hope something hits. This strategy isn't particularly artful, but it's safe. At the end of the day, the lesson is taught, the content is shared, and the knowledge is mastered—if not by all students, then by most.

But slicing through the center invariably flattens the feedback loop. If everyone is moving in the same direction, doing the same thing in the same way, then students become secondary to subjects. It's why the kids at Rama found themselves shut out at their regular schools. For them, like so many others, the learning experience felt strangely impersonal. Instead of a circle forming around teachers and students, there was a flat line connecting content and tasks. Forget about two-way communication or collaborative give-and-take. In a classroom sized for one—one task, one voice, one way—there's hardly room for two.

This brings us back to creativity. Eventually, today's students will become tomorrow's workforce. But we can't reasonably expect kids to bootleg the next product sensation if they've spent their entire academic careers bogged down by drudgery. Creativity gets tossed to the wayside when the only "right" way to travel is down a single road that's already been paved. Too much of today's instruction is prescripted. Students don't need to think about their route anymore. They aren't asked to anticipate points of interest or imagine alternative destinations. They just have to get there—quickly, quietly, and without a whole lot of interference. The journey itself is mostly irrelevant. The point is to *arrive*.

The coverage crush won't stop until we figure out a way to systematically overhaul education in this country. But in the meantime, there's a creativity countermovement on the rise. It works within the limits of federal and state standards but finds room for expression inside the margins. As a result, the range and reach of curiosity and learning grows, making classroom conversations richer and more audible. But this isn't another piece of reform. There's no earth-shattering solution. In fact, the concept is so simple, it just might be genius.

GENIUS HOUR: RECLAIMING CREATIVITY IN CLASS

They're calling it Genius Hour. Inspired by the sideline projects pursued by employees at Google and 3M, some schools are starting to do the same. For roughly sixty minutes a week, teachers turn over control to their students and let them explore a topic of their choosing, from how solar panels work to the best running shoes for marathoners. Sometimes the focus is more defined, but exactly how students research and present their work is limited only by their interests and creativity.

Along the way, teachers act like project managers and provide feedforward to keep students on track. Regular check-ins with students maintain open lines of communication. Teachers might refine a concept, pose a challenge, or suggest a new research angle. They lead with questions, not judgments. The process feels just like a Pixar crit session that expands possibilities and closely resembles the open-ended, project-based learning used at Rama, with teachers serving as information guides. They point students in the right direction, then stand back and navigate from the side. Coverage is definitely not on the itinerary.

Part of the reason students feel successful is because they're held accountable. In Joy Kirr's seventh-grade English class at Thomas Middle School in Arlington Heights, Illinois, students are required to complete one-on-one conferencing, biweekly goal setting, and self-evaluation. The project culminates in a class-wide presentation with members of the school board and city council on hand. Other teachers require students to maintain weekly blogs to document their success and failure. The projects born out of Genius Hour meet the school's curriculum standards and align with national benchmarks for reading, writing, and communication.

Ultimately, believes Kirr, these accountability measures aren't about compliance but getting kids to take personal responsibility. "They're not going to have teachers to help them throughout life," she says. "They're going to be on their own." If a proper education lets students stand on their own two feet, then Genius Hour props them up by taking away the crutches. It promotes a slow but certain shift toward autonomy and puts the focus back on students, not subjects. (We'll learn more about feedforward and autonomy in chapter 6.)

When we tell kids where to look but not what to see, they become empowered to design and discover new worlds. "Students love the freedom to explore what they are passionate about instead of just doing the work they are assigned by the teacher," says Nicholas Provenzaro, an English teacher at Grosse Pointe South High School in Michigan and a Genius Hour evangelist. "That freedom is what motivates them to uncover big ideas and take ownership of their learning."

It's not hard to see why. From our earliest moments, we're hardwired for curiosity. Our endless appetite for wonder makes us perk up whenever we see something unusual or spectacular. It's the reason we become absorbed in a new museum exhibit or find potato chip factory tours interesting. (The free samples don't hurt, either.) The desire to know *why* steered Moses as an adult to the burning bush and Albert Einstein as a child to the study of magnetism. Wanting to know how stuff works helps us make sense of the world and allows us to find our place inside it.

Curiosity may very well be the hidden force behind creativity. It provides the fuel for the Genius Hour movement and its emphasis on student agency and mastery, not just testing and accountability. But the sheer excitement of learning that comes naturally to kids can only withstand so much. With every bland worksheet, rote assignment, and predictable exercise handed down by the creativity killers, kids are reprogrammed to be task oriented, not curious. Eventually, the joy of wonder is forgotten.

Some of this may have to do with America's culture of high-stakes testing, though the truth is probably more nuanced and complex. And yet this much seems clear: Today's students have become conditioned to seek the certainty and safety of right answers. That means they're less likely to ask questions, take risks, and test bold ideas. This regression hampers their ability to learn right now, and it may even jeopardize their capacity to innovate later on. If students don't marvel about things, they probably won't make things, either.

NOT IN THE BUSINESS OF CREATIVITY

But it's not just traditional schooling that squelches our curious spirit. Business does its share of damage, too. In a study of workers across sixteen industries, George Mason University psychologist Todd Kashdan and Merck KGaA found that 65 percent of respondents thought curiosity was essential in discovering new ideas. But virtually the same percentage of workers felt unable to ask questions or challenge assumptions on the job. To that point, 84 percent reported that their employers encouraged curiosity, but nearly 60 percent said they faced barriers to it at work. The apparent contradictions revealed a double standard among management: Leaders like the concept of curiosity a lot more than the practice of it.

That may be due to the power siloes often created in the workplace. Recall from chapter 1 the steps that Deloitte took to break down hierarchal practices of performance analysis. The company realized that a rear-facing view doesn't yield a clear picture of the employee's professional net worth. Rather than having its managers share feedback about the past, which can't be changed, Deloitte redesigned its system to be more fluid, shifted the center of gravity from top to bottom, and cushioned ratings with reflections. It adopted a feed-forward approach that Regenerates the talent it has. But to create the virtuous feedback cycle of autonomy, empowerment, and improvement, managers needed to do more listening and let employees do more talking.

That's a tough habit to kick. Kashdan's study ranked industries based on the levels of inquisitiveness, creativity, distress tolerance, and openness employees felt in their workplaces, with a mean score of 0–100. He found that in certain industries, like financial services (48.8) and health care (49.3), managers seemed bent on consolidating their power rather than distributing it. The silos softened for workers in entertainment (57.8) and household products (60.3), probably because their hypercompetitive reach for customers on the ground accelerated risk taking at the top.

But the most intriguing results occurred in K–12 education, which fared slightly better than half the industries surveyed but showed a penchant for playing it safe. That's something we might expect from highly automated fields producing goods and services, but not from a knowledge industry pushing ideas and ideals. Ultimately, the aim of education is to produce wisdom, not widgets. Despite receiving a steady influx of money, technology, and resources, the vast majority of schools today look the same as they did fifty years ago.

"Organizations promote innovation, yet punish failure," Kashdan says. "They cling to legacy structures and systems that that emphasize authority over inquiry and routine over resourcefulness." He's talking about the self-punishing habits of corporations, of course. But just for fun, try reading the first line again, this time substituting *school* for *organization*: *Schools punish failure.* Unfortunately, that refrain has become all too familiar nowadays.

NO SHORTCUT TO EUREKA

It would be a mistake, though, to believe that creativity is born only when our minds are at rest or when it's part of the workplace ethos. Those coveted "eureka" moments arrive only with hard work—lots of it. As one landmark study on creativity has shown, the difference between expert performers and normal adults reflects a lifelong period of deliberate practice to improve performance in a particular area. What seems like a sudden burst in creativity is more like a slow accretion. Small but significant changes in our habits and behavior, accumulating over time, become so charged that the creativity lid eventually pops off. In the end, there's no shortcut to eureka, just a long, plodding road.

When we follow the feedback trail, it's possible we'll discover something new—and maybe a little uncomfortable. The way we cross our arms in meetings? Put-offish. Think you're a team player? Not everyone on the team agrees. It's funny how differently we see ourselves after piecing together these fragments. We learn that we don't listen as well as we should, stand as straight as we should, eat as healthy as we should. Our carefully concealed shortcomings suddenly rise to the surface and, with them, the realization that maybe we aren't nearly as perfect as we once imagined.

You'd think those revelations would cut us down to size just a bit. But a surprising majority of people use the negativity as fuel for finding new opportunities. When feedforward is truly Authentic, giving a negative report can actually lead to *more* creativity, not less. Since many people, especially those with high levels of expertise, would prefer to remedy their shortcomings rather than accept them as fact, what began as a point of weakness may well become a source of wholeness. Instead of playing victim to their imperfections, these individuals choose the heroic path of self-determination, which is where creativity starts to breed.

That's what researchers at Columbia Business School found when they studied the real-time effects of nonverbal feedback on a group of young professionals. Asked to deliver a short speech about their dream job, participants sounded off as reactions from a panel of judges rolled in: approving nods and smiles for standout presenters, dismayed head shakes and frowns for uninspiring talkers. Immediately after their presentations, participants were told to complete a self-report that captured their post-performance moods. As you might expect, the people who perceived signs of encouragement felt upbeat and proud; those who sensed disapproval did not.

To see how these emotions played out, researchers followed up with another task. They gave each of the presenters a basic kit of supplies—some colored felt, glue, and construction paper—and told them to make something artistic. The creative quality of their work would be evaluated by the same panel of judges who offered nonverbal feedback about their dream job speeches. Just moments after getting one top-to-bottom appraisal, these participants were about to get another.

What happened next surprised the researchers. The people who initially received poor reviews for their career talks ended up drawing higher ratings for their art samples than those who felt praised. Their products were, by comparison, more expressive, colorful, unusually designed, and original. This turn of events led researchers to conclude that disappointment had become a catalyst for determination. The initial setback provoked a sharper inward focus and willingness to tackle more difficult and creative artistic expressions, spurred on by the alpha waves emanating from the brain's right hemisphere.

UNLEASH WHAT'S INSIDE

There's a lesson here for performance evaluators of all types, whether it's teachers assessing the work of their students or supervisors measuring the productivity of their team. Getting others to do their best work happens when we manage from a point of detached connection: close enough to matter, but too far to meddle. People need assurances that their work is meaningful and that their bosses care enough to notice. (Think back to the Hawthorne effect from chapter 1.) But when we take to prescribing solutions instead of inviting suggestions, we thwart the natural genius of the team—whether that "team" happens to organize inside a board room, a classroom, or around the dining room.

A lot depends on the message itself. When feedback insists on right answers, offers little or no choice, or dictates performance goals, it plays a zero-sum game. Only one view can prevail—the feedback giver's. To accept a second view would be to diminish the first. That's what happens when the dynamics are about control, but they don't have to be. When we embrace feedforward, power is diffused, not hoarded. It places greater value on curiosity over conformity, inquiry over indoctrination, autonomy over authority. What we think matters less than what others already know. And if we want to help, the best thing we can do sometimes is step aside and let them discover it for themselves.

To really fix our feedback, we need to speak in a way that lets people hear their own internal frequencies. It's what Elad Segev did, and what many of the businesses surveyed by Todd Kashdan did not. Helping other people tune their own dials is what's driving the Genius Hour movement in schools and the speculative projects at truly innovative companies. They're teaching the rest of us that creativity is something to be unleashed, not imposed.

But to locate and release that kind of original energy, people need to develop a keener sense of their interiors. Holding up a mirror for them to gaze into is powerful, but only once they've cultivated the habits that lead to self-awareness. The next chapter shows how.

4

Consciousness

With just minutes to go before the start of the 2014 NFL season, the Seattle Seahawks look fully charged. Judging by the electric atmosphere at CenturyLink Field, so are sixty-seven thousand thunderous fans. As the team prepares for pregame introductions, the decibel of the crowd rises from a low rumble to a full-throated holler, making it nearly impossible to hear the person one seat over. Not that it matters much, since all eyes are glued to the spectacle taking place down on the field.

On cue, a cascade of fireworks erupts from two giant columns just as fifty-three players explode from a cavernous concrete tunnel. They dart out quickly, first the backup squad and then the starting line, thumping their bodies and brandishing their helmets like combat warriors. Actually, with their dark navy uniforms streaked in neon green, they seem more like futuristic space rangers from another planet. Except what's about to happen is no fantasy.

For the past few seasons, the Seahawks have been one of the NFL's most dominant teams. They've won consecutive division and conference titles—no small feat in the age of free agency and the salary cap. Their stingy defense allowed the fewest points of any team in the league for four seasons in a row. And they've appeared in two of the last four Super Bowls, winning it all in 2014. They are disciplined, fearsome, and fast. Tonight, the Seahawks completely manhandle their opponent, the Green Bay Packers. At the end of regulation, the score is 36–16. It was never a contest.

Without a doubt, the Seahawks are well coached and possess incredible talent. Their athleticism is superb. Their execution is nearly flawless. That alone gives them a strong competitive edge, but it doesn't quite make them elite. Off the field, there's not much difference between them and the other thirty-one NFL teams. The Seahawks train rigorously and condition their bodies to perfection, but so does the rest of the league. The team lifts weights like everybody else, watches game film like everybody else, and takes reps like everybody else. But when it comes to winning, the Seahawks are most certainly *not* like everybody else. They flat-out outperform everyone.

You'd never know it just from watching the games, but there's a hidden element at work. The Seahawks don't just train for physical advantage. They also tune themselves for mental toughness. It began with the arrival of Coach Pete Carroll, who teaches his players to believe that victory starts with an inside game—not just how the body performs but also how the mind thinks. To get players to buy in, Carroll added a secret weapon: one man within the organization who could take the science of psychology to another level. And tonight, as the team racks up nearly four hundred yards in total offense and stifles the Packers' game-breaking threats, Michael Gervais is there, watching.

Gervais is not a football jock. He isn't one of the team's twenty-six coaches. He's not even a member of the Seahawks' front office. Gervais is a trained psychologist specializing in the science of high performance. With wavy black hair and an easy smile, Gervais doesn't fit the NFL coach stereotype. He speaks calmly, almost soothingly, when describing the chaotic and pressured world of high-stakes environments, where there's little room for mistakes, hesitation, or timidity.

It's a world he knows well. A former competitive surfer, Gervais has worked with Hall of Fame and MVP athletes from virtually every major professional sport, including three-time gold medalist Kerri Walsh Jennings, the beach volleyball star, and space-diver Felix Baumgartner, who in 2012 broke the sound barrier when he jumped out of a capsule twenty-five miles above the earth. If you get thrills from surfing eighty-foot waves or jumping forty-foot spines on skis in the Canadian backcountry, chances are you've heard of Michael Gervais. "The people I work with thrive in off-terrain engagements, where the coaching is limited, the consequences are severe, and the intensity is strong," he says.

As far as high-intensity environments go in traditional sports, the NFL might top the list. The game is played fast and furiously. It's physically brutal from end to end, with athletes crashing into each other at high speeds on every down. And with a compact regular season that runs just sixteen games, every win or loss carries huge stakes. The leader board can be completely up-ended from week to week. With teams' fortunes rising or falling on any given Sunday, you never know who's going to come out on top—which is why it's a little surprising at first to see a guy like Gervais working with a professional football club.

On the surface, it would seem that the game is played and won on the merits of brute force, not delicate calculation. You don't expect three-hundred-pound defensive backs to suddenly withdraw into blissful introspection while trying to topple the opposing team's linemen. But that's *exactly* where Carroll wants his players to be and why he introduced them to Gervais in 2011. Both men are gripped by rugged environments that demand inner trust, letting go, refined skill, and the interconnectivity of social flow. They understand that success means keeping the mind in the chaotic present when all it wants to do is retreat to the comfort of safety.

To achieve that kind of focus, Gervais blends the science of high-performance mind-set training with state-of-the-art brain mapping and ancient traditions of mindfulness. His program is built around individualized performance plans that allow people to discover their personal best by fully engaging their minds and brains. But instead of talking Xs and Os, Gervais develops the strategies and mental skills of those who are invested in finding mastery.

That unfolds through a cognitive developmental approach aimed at understanding who a person is and what he or she can become. It's driven by relationships-based coaching that enables individuals to uncover their personal best, a practice that runs deep in the team's football operations. "It's the most fascinating culture I have ever been able to witness," Gervais said of the Seahawks. "There is a relentless approach, driven by Coach Carroll, to the idea that relationships matter."

For those relationships to be truly effective, though, they need to be authentic, not just transactional. They emerge from a shared vision of excellence that is established around broad and binding team values. Gervais helps train players and coaches to tap their closest-held beliefs about who they are and how they can achieve their best within those overarching goals. The result, once honed, is a high regard for the work of others and self. "When we can trust each other that our intent is right, that becomes one of the most powerful accelerants of communication and output," he says.

In these conversations, you don't hear much talk about winning—which is sort of ironic, since the Seahawks tend to do plenty of that. It's a striking omission, especially in the world of professional sports, where our view of achievement usually slides toward the end product, not process. When the final whistle blows, success is measured by the number of completions thrown, sacks tallied, yards rushed—and, of course, wins.

But there's no real mention of that, not by Gervais or the coaching staff. "Winning is not the vision. The vision is for people to become their personal best," says Gervais. The Seahawks' playbook calls for deep reflection and presence by every player, from the starting tailback down to the third-string safety. "Winning is the extension of people competing to be and do their very best together." Given the team's spectacular triumphs, it's hard to argue with that.

FEEDBACK: THE INSIDE GAME

Until now, we've explored the broken nature of traditional feedback and how feedforward can REPAIR it. Whether it's based on an approach that improves decision making or unleashes creativity, these fixes are applied by outsiders—a manager, a teacher, a close friend. Their feedback is meant to change us from the outside in, mostly by pushing *their* suggestions for how we might go about improving our personal or professional flaws. That means that much of the feedback we receive forces us to face outward in the direction of another person. They're the ones leading the way. We're just coming along for the ride.

Something remarkable begins to happen, however, when we turn this process inside out and start leading from within. It's here that we come across our own internal channels—the quiet but powerful self-knowledge we hold about our passions, dislikes, secret hopes, and unspoken concerns. It's the fragile parts of ourselves we know but don't dare share, sometimes even with those closest to us. We don't allow them to penetrate our self-concealing shells.

Come to think of it, there's really no one else in the world who knows us the way we do. Others may see what we know, but only we know what we see—and we see more than anyone else. No one can access the hazy parts of our deep consciousness. So if feedback is supposed to bring about a change in behavior, and behavioral change starts with a shift in mind-set, then it turns out that we, and no one else, hold the best view of our own performance. After all, we're the ultimate insiders.

If we're courageous enough to look inward, we'll discover that the most honest feedback we may ever receive comes from within, not beyond. That's not to say that we can change all by ourselves or even that we should. Listening to another voice can be instructive. But responding to our own voice can be transformative. Well before we receive someone else's design, we need to have an acute sense of our own space—the job we want to do, the person we want to be. When we begin to trace the inner linings of our true selves, we come to realize what lies inside. That's the moment we make feedforward an inside game.

The goal here isn't talking but tuning—an active examination of our own interiors to better understand how we can contribute to our success and to the success of others. This feedforward approach isn't formal, prescheduled, or tied up in procedure. There's no hired coach, checklist, or training manual. Instead, we look to the future by finding our inner voice and listening more closely to what it tells us.

That's exactly how Michael Gervais helps his clients find mastery, whether they're professional athletes, extreme-sport enthusiasts, military personnel, or business leaders. He asks a lot of questions that help performers establish mindfulness, recalling the things they remember feeling, thinking, seeing—even smelling—in the moment of pursuit. This trains them to be consciously aware of themselves and their environment. "It allows them to adjust eloquently to adversity," says Gervais, "since they know the triggers that prevent them from reaching their best self."

Once we're present in the moment, the focus shifts toward potential: What does excellence look like, and how can it be captured? Maybe it's leading your division in sales year after year or producing the highest-grossing films of the decade. It could be priming your children to receive a shiny college acceptance letter or helping your students earn the highest math scores in the district. Whatever the goal, most people tend to think about excellence in terms of their own accomplishments: accolades received, bonuses netted, promotions won. The more of it we have, the better we are. It's a rather self-absorbing picture of peak performance.

It's also highly unstable. Even with exquisite preparation and execution, there are things that we simply can't control. We don't plan for last-minute surprises or unexpected curveballs. They just happen. And when they do, we realize how much we need other people and how our success really depends on them. Especially in today's hypercollaborative environments, where the work of individuals gets folded into group products, there aren't many instances when success can be so narrowly and selectively defined.

But there's another measure of success, one that is more constant and steady. Instead of trying to stand out with personal achievements, we grab hold of common values. These are team-driven understandings of what defines success and personal best. They round out the organization's self-made portrait of performance at a high level, based upon the attitudes and actions that form the aspirations of the group. As a performance mind-set, this view encourages thinking in the plural. *What does our team stand for? What are our larger purposes and priorities?* When individuals scale success at this level, their achievement isn't just a personal triumph. It's a victory for the entire team. It widens the boundaries of achievement.

These are the kinds of questions we ask with feedforward. It causes us to realign our beliefs and behaviors with a team focus, leading to bigger results and deeper relationships. For the Seahawks, that balance brought about cohesiveness, communication, and ultimately, a league championship. For the rest of us, it could be the key to optimizing our personal best in our everyday work and relationships. But achieving success through self-awareness means that we have to challenge some old assumptions, starting with how feedback ought to sound and start.

SELF-TALK: COACHING FROM INSIDE

As we've noted, traditional feedback moves from the outside in. It develops in other people's hands before making its way into our heads. They're the ones who tend to initiate the conversation and do most of the talking, while we sit back and sweat it out. After years of being conditioned to this style of feedback, we've come to believe that it must inevitably follow that line—originate on the outside, then work its way in. Wrong. That may be part of the travel path, but it's not the origination point. Feedback didn't start with someone else. It began with you.

Think back to your last high-stakes encounter. Was it a big presentation you made to senior management? A callback interview for the dream job you've desperately wanted? Maybe it was talking to your teens about the perils of underage drinking, or asking out that cute brunette for a first date. If you're like most people, you probably entered that moment with a sickening feeling of self-doubt. *Can I really pull this off? What if I collapse under pressure?* You may have even begun to write off your prospects before actually trying.

But then something happened. Just as the hesitation started to creep in, a small, reassuring voice piped up. It had a familiar sound, like your own. The voice was yours. It spoke in hushed tones, just audible enough for you to hear. It reminded you that you're prepared, practiced, and equal to the task. It walked you through the steps of execution, exactly the way you've done it before or planned to do it now. It told you not to worry so much. As the voice spoke, you may have even begun to speak with it. Gradually, all that doubt, once unconquerable, started to ebb away.

Psychologists have a term for this. It's called *self-talk*, or the conversation we tend to have with ourselves during moments of critical importance. We tend to caricature self-talkers, from the absentminded professor muttering high-brow mumbo jumbo to the oddball on the subway having an animated one-way conversation. We apologize for "talking to ourselves" in public places and feel a hint of embarrassment when someone catches us in the act of speaking when no one else is around.

But move past the social stigma, and there's quite a bit of evidence to suggest that self-talk is actually a good thing. For starters, it enhances attention on the present by setting our focus on the task at hand. This allows us to talk our way around distraction, screening out the stimuli that divert us from doing the right thing, at the right time. Imagine the self-talk of a new driver preparing to hit the road: *OK, fasten seat belt, check mirrors, turn on ignition . . . now pull out in reverse slowly, hands in position . . .*

Self-talk also helps us regulate effort and make decisions about what to do and when to do it. Thinking about squeezing in a quick trip to the grocery store before getting your kid from school? *Well, if I leave now, I'll probably hit traffic, and the checkout lines move so slowly around 3 p.m. . . . . I'd better go straight to school and just hit the store on the way back.* That self-talk may have saved Johnny from being the last kid to get picked up in the carpool line—again.

Most important, the self-talk we practice helps us control cognitive and emotional reactions, serving as a mental restraint that stops us from making choices we'll later regret. Remember the time you nearly exploded at a member of your sales team for offering a ridiculous suggestion during a strategy session? Just before you blew your top, some self-talk held you back. *Don't yell at Greg, even though he's a moron. You don't want people thinking that you're not a team player . . . they might even take his side, you know, out of sympathy. Just sit tight and keep quiet, OK?*

There's a unifying quality to these features. With self-talk, we unmute our inner coaching voice. It's a self-guiding force that keeps us on track, whether we're walking through the steps of a familiar procedure or just reminding ourselves not to step into an uncomfortable situation. Without a clipboard or a spreadsheet, our coaching voice is there to make sure we navigate with caution, reason, and restraint. Because it's intuitive and self-produced, it might just be the most honest feedback we ever receive. And with its inside-out trajectory, it allows us to initiate feedforward that starts with us, not someone else.

But self-talk isn't just a powerful way to handle our own decisions and emotions. It turns out to be a pretty effective tool for managing other people, too. Researchers at the University of North Carolina at Chapel Hill investigated the impact of self-talk among effective and ineffective managers to see if inner tuning had anything to do with their executive skills. To test the correlation, they assembled a pool of 189 senior managers recognized for strong leadership skills and creativity. Their task: Write letters to themselves about their accomplishments and plans for the future.

Based on these written samples, a group of raters evaluated the language used by managers for signs of constructive or dysfunctional self-talk. Letters that rated high in constructive self-talk proved to be insightful, thoughtfully composed, self-reflective, and motivational in nature. The constructive self-talkers saw themselves as capable, confident leaders who would ultimately achieve their desired goals.

For example, one statement of constructive self-talk read, "You are good at what you do, so you are going to start giving yourself credit—publicly. And the next time someone compliments you on something, do not brush them off so that all they can say is a quick 'thank-you'—take it all in." Self-talkers who fell into this category also tended to produce letters that received high marks for creativity, originality, and leadership skills.

Then there were the dysfunctional self-talkers—the managers who, by and large, shied away from challenges instead of facing them. Their letters revealed a strong aversion to adversity and a pessimistic outlook toward change of any kind. One letter from a dysfunctional self-talker went like this: "And how's the mess at the office? Still canceling appointments or showing up in the wrong meetings? Hope you can handle your schedule a little better now. . . ."

The tone that managers used to conclude their letters also had a lot to do with their type of self-talk. Constructive self-talkers ended on a positive and encouraging note, expressing confidence in their ability to deliver strong results. By contrast, letters featuring dysfunctional self-talk finished with doom and gloom predictions by managers who sensed that their prospects for success—not to mention those of the companies they led—were slim.

Not surprisingly, raters scored the letters from constructive self-talkers much higher than those from the dysfunctional group. No surprise there, especially considering that the self-talking managers happened to be high achievers in general. But the rib wasn't the actual letters—it was how these scores related to measures of the managers' *actual effectiveness*. When researchers correlated the ratings from managers' self-talk with indexes for leadership, creativity, originality, and perceptions of job strain, they found that the constructive self-talkers ranked higher in every category. *Every one.* Self-talk didn't just make them more mindful. It turned them into better managers.

PHANTOM PRACTICE

All of this may have something to do with what neurologists call "motor imagery," or the mental simulation of physical actions. Even if you don't know the term, chances are you've experienced the phenomenon. Motor imagery causes us to feel that we've done something without really having done it— "it" happened in our imaginations. Brain scans show that people use the same neurological networks whether they are actually moving or simply envisioning movement. Just thinking about the step-by-step sequence of an action is enough to reactivate it inside our working memory, the part of our brains we turn to for information recall and execution.

That means that reviewing the steps of an activity over and over can have the same cognitive effect as physical practice—and even lead to similar improvements in performance. Physical therapists have used motor imagery to help subacute stroke victims regain strength, range of motion, and postural control in tandem with actual rehab interventions. There's even documented evidence that motor imagery can yield clinical improvements in patients with spinal cord injury, Parkinson's disease, and intractable pain. It's phantom practice, but the effects are real.

But if motor imagery is the back door, then self-talk is the key. It unlocks a serious, self-inspecting view of performance that doesn't overanalyze, paralyze, or dramatize. The clarity it brings puts us on a straight and practical path toward success. We walk ourselves through the motions, note the sequence, and plot our advance. It's a remarkably simple and intuitive way to navigate around the fear or limitations that hold us back. And it's another prime example of how feedforward becomes an inside game every time we access and act on information we already possess.

There's good reason to believe self-talk can make a difference, especially if it's incorporated into a cycle of thought and action. First comes forethought, when we set a goal for ourselves and make a plan for how to get there. That's followed by action, when we enact the plan to the best of our ability. Last comes self-reflection, when we carefully evaluate what we've done and adjust our plan for the next encounter. The target can be profound, like a behavioral change, or much simpler, like a recreational hobby. When researchers studied the accuracy of students learning how to throw darts in gym class, they found that the ones who assimilated this pattern into practice made their marks more often than those who didn't.

It also seemed to work for more rigorous and physically demanding tasks. In a study of elite sprinters, runners who spoke key words to themselves during specific intervals tended to outperform their competitors. They used verbal cues like *push* during the acceleration phase of the sprint, *heel* during the maximum-speed phase, and *claw* during the endurance phase. Each word carried a specific motor message tailored precisely for the moment. (If you're a runner, you already knew that.) When they called out the signals, the athletes ran faster. The self-talk refocused them on fundamentals, ultimately driving better performance.

THE MINDFUL HABIT

What's going on here has as much to do with the mind as it does the body. Getting ourselves primed for performance requires a certain amount of physical discipline—diet and training are key, especially for high-endurance tasks—but there's a whole component of mindfulness that's revolutionizing how we prepare for and perform on the grand stage. Rooted in ancient Buddhist traditions, the practice has recently gained mainstream appeal. Researchers are touting the game-changing health and lifestyle benefits. And it's providing a competitive edge to performance of all types—whether it's on the field or in the boardroom, the kind we do by ourselves or with the help of others.

Depending on who you ask, mindfulness can mean any number of things. You might hear anything from meditation to relaxation to sunrise yoga on the beach. In experimental psychology, the word is more rigorously defined as controlled attentiveness, a deliberate awareness of what is happening in the present moment. In the late 1970s, Jon Kabat-Zinn, a molecular biologist and founding director of the Center for Mindfulness in Medicine, Health Care and Society at the University of Massachusetts Medical School, coined a non-enlightenment version: the awareness that arises through paying attention on purpose, in the present moment, and nonjudgmentally (sounds about right).

But however we choose to understand the term, there's no denying its positive effects on mind *and* body. In recent years, scientists have found associations between mindfulness and physical health—especially for weight control, with people who eat mindfully during mealtime tending to consume less food. Similarly, in a study of Chinese college students, individuals who were randomly assigned to participate in a mindfulness meditation intervention showed lower rates of depression and anxiety; reported fewer incidents of fatigue, anger, and stress; and demonstrated greater attention, self-regulation, and immunoreactivity than those in a control group.

There are reported psychological benefits as well. In the aftermath of Hurricane Katrina, the costliest natural disaster in U.S. history, researchers studied a group of New Orleans mental health workers who dealt directly with victims to see whether mindful practices could change their reported levels of psychological distress. It did. At the end of an eight-week mindfulness intervention, workers showed significant reduction in their levels of post-traumatic stress and anxiety, even though the psychological scars were still painful and fresh.

The health benefits are so real that it's causing managed-care providers to take note. Aetna, one of the country's largest medical insurers, launched a mindfulness study in 2010 in collaboration with Duke University to explore new pathways for stress reduction and prevention. Out of 239 Aetna employees from its California and Connecticut offices, two-thirds were randomly assigned to mindfulness-based classes and programs, while the rest were assigned to a control group receiving only conventional treatments.

The results were striking. Participants in the mind-body stress-reduction treatment group showed a 36 percent decrease in stress levels, compared to only an 18 percent reduction for the control group. Those receiving mind-body interventions also saw significant improvements in various heart-rate measurements, suggesting that their bodies were better able to manage stress. Aetna found the results so encouraging that it now offers a version of the program to all of its employees as well as its self-insured commercial customers. Beyond promoting better health, mindfulness can also pad the bottom line. (After all, people who are less stressed end up being healthier—*and* cheaper to insure.)

The mindfulness trend is catching on with corporations as well. Companies like Green Mountain Coffee Roasters and Intel offer mindfulness programs and retreats to employees and their families. To create a more mindful workplace, General Mills developed a voluntary job-embedded mindfulness training program that has served more than five hundred employees and ninety senior leaders since it launched in 2006. And Target started building a network of "meditation merchants" that has trained more than one thousand employees in mindful techniques.

While the specifics of these initiatives differ from company to company, the basic goals remain the same: improve employee focus, sharpen decision-making capabilities, and unleash more creativity around the workplace. It's feedforward that Expands our way of thinking, and the results speak for themselves.

STRESSED OUT BY SCHOOL

But the strongest push for mindfulness is happening in schools, and for good reason: Kids today are simply stressed out. As a nation, we're even on record for it. Every year since 2007, the American Psychological Association (APA) has commissioned a nationwide study to examine the state of stress across the country and understand its impact. The Stress in America survey measures attitudes and perceptions of stress among the general public and identifies leading sources of stress, common behaviors used to manage stress, and the impact of stress on our lives.

In 2009, the APA confirmed what many have long suspected: A significant number of children and teenagers are suffering from stress, with school being a leading cause. Nearly half—45 percent—of the teens ages thirteen to seventeen who were surveyed said they felt stressed by pressures at school. Twenty-six percent of tweens from ages eight to twelve claimed they "worried more" than in the past year, while 44 percent of students between eight and seventeen reported that "doing well in school" was an ongoing source of concern.

There was more. Alongside the spike in adolescent stress, the survey showed an alarming disconnect between child attitudes and parental perceptions. On some of the most serious stress indicators, particularly those related to school, parents understood the warning signs to be far less ominous than what their children actually reported. Only 28 percent of parents thought their teens' stress had increased over the past year, while just 17 percent of parents perceived a rise in tween angst. Whereas 29 percent of children ages thirteen to seventeen claimed to worry about getting into a good college, only 5 percent of parents felt like their children carried that burden.

Parents didn't fare much better when it came to noticing the physiological effects of stress on kids. Children were three times more likely to report stress-related sleeping difficulties in the past month than their parents observed (45 percent to 13 percent, respectively) and were four times more likely to report eating too much or too little in the past month than parents cared to admit, by a margin of 34 percent to 8 percent. It makes you wonder if the divide between what children feel and what parents see could itself be a silent cause of childhood stress.

So what can be done? Dialing down standards or reducing the academic workload may relieve the stress, but it won't breed success, especially in the long run. Placing outsized demands and expectations on children may be harmful, but so is gutting them. We can't expect to raise soft kids into resilient adults without a little stress along the way. Insulating them from relatively minor stressors when they're young will only make it harder for them to confront and control the major stressors when they're older—jobs, money, marriage, and kids of their own. (Chapter 6 shows how feedforward can build greater resilience in adults.)

If we can't (or shouldn't) eliminate all stress from school, then the least we can do is help students manage it proactively. For that, mindfulness turns out to be quite the stress suppressant. In the past decade, there has been a surge in mindful trainings and techniques at schools around the country, helping kids tap into all that brain power they're supposed to use in class by training their minds and moods to increase focus, decrease stress, and gain emotional resilience.

One of the leading sources of school-based mindfulness is MindUP, a training program that combines cognitive neuroscience, positive psychology, and mindful awareness to help children achieve academic success. Founded by Academy Award–winning actress Goldie Hawn, MindUP uses brain-based lesson plans to help students self-regulate their behavior and mindfully engage in focused concentration. Currently, its curriculum is used by an estimated 13,500 teachers and 405,000 students across the United States, and its training programs have reached more than a thousand counseling and youth centers around the world.

MindUP trainings consist of fifteen lessons that help kids learn how to quiet their minds by understanding their brains. There's a lot of neuroscience mixed in, and kids become well acquainted with the features and functions of the brain's amygdala, hippocampus, and prefrontal cortex, but it's bundled in a way that's kid friendly. (The curriculum even comes with a handy chime that teachers play to create calm and focus. I still have mine.) The goal is to help children improve their academic performance by reinforcing life-enhancing habits like resilience, empathy, and self-control—what today might be called character strengths.

So far, all signs point to success. Fourth and fifth graders who participated in the twelve-week program showed an improvement in stress regulation and cognitive control, a decrease in depression, and enhanced pro-social behaviors. Eighty-two percent experienced greater optimism and self-concept, while 24 percent reported lower levels of aggression and anger. Besides the character benefits, MindUP even helped students produce a 15 percent gain in their math achievement scores, showing that soft skills can translate into hard gains.

There are signs that the mindfulness movement is spreading internationally as well. In the first large-scale experiment of its kind, researchers at three major universities in the United Kingdom (including Oxford) have joined forces to examine the link between mindfulness and stress reduction in teens. The three-year trial will examine whether and how mindfulness improves the mental resilience of teenagers, followed by a two-year evaluation of the most effective ways to train teachers to deliver mindfulness classes to students.

In choosing to study teens, a population notorious for its rash decision making and impulsive behavior, researchers hope to show how mindfulness can promote better mental resilience and self-control than traditional school-based interventions, which tend to be reactive and punitive. Instead of lashing out at teens for their erratic and exasperating behavior, we might actually help them get a handle on their emotions *before* they explode into something that turns out to be stupid, dangerous, or worse. If mindfulness can tame the teenage beast, we'll all be a lot safer and saner. And feedforward can help.

DEVELOPING AN INSIDE GAME

By now it should be clear why developing an inside game is so critical to our success. From creating stronger performances in sports to implementing more deliberate practices in businesses and schools, self-tuning brings us closer to the source of our quiet potential by helping us listen to our own frequencies. Unlike traditional feedback, which takes an outside-in approach, feedforward develops inside-out, starting with an honest self-appraisal of our performance and priorities. With feedback, we look back at what we've done. With feedforward, we listen in to what we can still achieve.

Getting there is a lot harder. To experience greater presence in our everyday encounters, our inside game needs a playbook. The mind needs to be trained to think with new rules. Here are five:

Describe, don't prescribe.

One thing at a time.

Treat all moments as equals.

Make it stick.

Trust yourself.

1   Describe, Don't Prescribe

When it comes time to self-evaluate, we tend to exaggerate our sins and shortcomings. That's the liability of closeness—we may be the ultimate insiders, but that proximity can also cause nearsightedness. We're so close to the action that it's almost impossible to have a clear-eyed view of actual events. What we think we're seeing may be a crude distortion, for good or bad. Knowing that, it's much more productive—and authentic—to describe the problem itself, rather than prescribe ways to fix it.

Just as you feel yourself begin to agonize over a challenging situation at work or home, pull back. Place yourself to the side for a moment and describe the scene: What do you feel, think, or see just before or during the encounter? Be precise and nonjudgmental. Don't give in to unwarranted self-critique. By increasing our awareness and shedding our preconceptions, we separate the real from the imagined and sketch only what our senses tell us.

One effective way to do that is by labeling our emotions. That's what researchers at UCLA discovered when they studied the reactions of people with spider phobias as they approached a dreaded arachnid. Participants were told to label their anxiety (verbalize the fear), think differently about the spider (what psychologists call reappraisal), or distract themselves entirely (look away at something else). The group that verbalized their fears showed the fewest signs of reactivity, suggesting that "naming the monster" can be a powerful way to sidestep the nightmare scenarios we all too often conjure up.

2   One Thing at a Time

The world today is more hyperactive than ever. We're constantly in motion—toggling between apps, talking and texting at once, handling the home front at work and managing work worries at home. We know the drawbacks of multitasking—it's harder to think, learn, and recall information—but recent findings show that it may even hamper our ability to rapidly switch *between* tasks. Researchers were amazed to discover that high multitaskers—those who reported using multiple forms of media simultaneously—took longer to switch tasks when prompted than those with lower multitasking tendencies.

The high multitaskers had a more difficult time filtering useful information from useless distractions. That caused them to treat every detail with equal importance and ignore cues that might have otherwise helped them rank and order the flow of information. There's also evidence that suggests that even *sitting* in direct view of a multitasker can inhibit performance. If that leads to a drop-off in productivity, then multitasking can turn out to be more of a time-killer than a time-saver.

This is where feedforward can help. By demanding deep focus on the task at hand, it prevents the kind of attention loss that comes with task hopping. Devoting ourselves to one thing brings renewed energy, clarity, and purpose to every encounter. To turn multitasking into single-tasking, choose one item from your crammed agenda and take it for a deep dive. Or rank and rotate your list of priorities so that several action items can be independently explored with greater attentiveness over the course of a week. You'll be amazed by how much smarter and better your work becomes.

3 Treat All Moments as Equals

If you've ever let stage fright get in the way of self-reflection, you're not alone. We allow the enormity of performance to pull us from our inner thoughts. But Michael Gervais, the high-performance psychologist, doesn't buy into the idea of big moments. "There's no such thing as a 'big moment'— it's just another moment," he says. "And we have an obligation to meet every moment with equal intensity and purpose."

While certain encounters produce a stronger fear factor than others—a pitch to senior management might register a higher "awe score" than, say, a presentation within your team—the difference is relational. We exaggerate the stakes of one moment and downplay the significance of another, but the two are qualitatively the same. When we treat all moments as equals, we don't let artificiality clog up our inner cool.

4 Make It Stick

Many have accepted the idea of an "emotional set point," or that some people are just more wired for stress than others and there's not much they can do about it. Not so. Researchers showed that even high-stress employees at a biotech firm who practiced mindfulness for thirty minutes a day managed to shift their emotional state and even raised their immune levels after just eight weeks. They literally changed their mood meters by engaging in routine acts of self-check.

That's encouraging, but building an inside game requires more than just a time slot. To endure, it needs a total habit makeover. As Charles Duhigg has shown, breaking old habits and starting new ones is practically primordial; it follows a loop of behavioral cues and rewards. We start with a craving for a reward, which gets introduced by some cue—a "trigger." That generates a behavioral response, which in turn creates a brand-new neural lane inside the brain's superhighway. At first, the connection is fragile and nonpermanent. But it grows stronger and more concrete every time we circle the loop of see-want-do, until finally it hardens into a fixed and dedicated path. Reward, cue, action, repeat—and voilà, we've formed a new habit.

The benefits of inside-out feedback compound naturally. When we achieve greater presence in everyday moments, we experience greater clarity, productivity, satisfaction, and finally, happiness. These are the rewards. All that's needed to complete our habit-forming loop is a cue. For that, create a "trigger" for mindfulness by ritualizing everyday actions into reminders. It could be anything from flicking on the light at your desk to grabbing a cup of coffee from the break room. Making those moments part a mindfulness routine is how we create the time, space, and frequency to establish a new normal.

5 | Trust Yourself

In her book *A Return to Love*, Marianne Williamson urges us to recognize our power and potential. She writes, "Our deepest fear is not that we are inadequate. Our deepest fear is that we are powerful beyond measure. It is our light, not our darkness that most frightens us. We ask ourselves, 'Who am I to be brilliant, gorgeous, talented, fabulous?' Actually, who are you not to be? You are a child of God. Your playing small does not serve the world." It doesn't serve our best interests, either.

Listening to your own voice means learning to trust yourself again. With so much feedback coming from other people—our supervisor, district evaluator, even our mother-in-law—we seem to have forgotten that we're the ones with the courtside seats. No one knows us the way we do. But we can't generate our own feedforward if we play small with our potential. We're capable of doing a lot more than we think, but only if we summon the courage to listen and act.

■ ■ ■

Performance, by its very nature, tends to be measured by how it looks on the outside. But optimal performance hinges on an inside game—the ability to listen carefully to the quiet signals of our inner voice. From mindfulness that improves team performance, personal health, and student achievement to self-talk that helps us run marathons and better businesses, feedforward increases our attention and presence. Discovering our personal best is one thing. Diffusing it within the home, a school, or an organization is another. To do that, we must turn suppliers into stakeholders, something that happens when feedforward spreads throughout teams.

5

Teams

The first thing you notice about Stagen Leadership Academy is the glass panels. They're spotless. Stretching from floor to ceiling, they arch slightly at the center, forming a concave enclosure that sets apart nearly ten thousand square feet of meeting and office space from an adjacent lobby. The effect is quite dramatic, as though you're standing outside a life-size snow globe. Compared to the nearby bustle of people and parcel deliveries, the scene on the other side of the glass looks quiet, almost serene.

Just past the welcome area is a dining nook, replete with a black granite-top bar and kitchenette. The cozy lighting, earthy tones, and plush seating makes you wonder if a barista might suddenly pop up with your latte order. Actually, they serve a lot more than coffee at Stagen. A chef prepares breakfast and lunch on-site, plus an array of snacks throughout the day. (When I visit, there's fresh guacamole, chips, and salsa standing by in the break room.)

The foyer design is sleek and modern, bathed in soft light. An open floor plan allows for lots of chance encounters and casual run-ins. Rooms are designed with chic minimalism—neutral colors, flexible seating, and a few potted plants. But beneath the contemporary facade, there's something *old* about the place, an appreciation of time and things from long ago. The polished hardwoods hail from Virginia oaks dating back to the late 1800s. Meeting spaces are named for the ancient Greek gods, like the cavernous training room ("Athena") and intimate collaboration work space ("Apollo"). Even the art decor is vintage.

But for Rand Stagen, the company's namesake and managing director, the modish furnishings say a lot about the mission, too. Time awareness is the company's beating heart, something that informs its beliefs, values, and practices. Pilot trim, with a firm jaw and intense brown eyes, Rand is the lead visionary of the academy, which he cofounded in 1999. He's also its chief evangelist. "We're not in the business of short-term," he declares, gesturing to the time-honored symbols around him. "We don't ask our people how far they can go, but how far they can *see*."

That means looking beyond the here and now toward a faraway goal. Playing the long game is critical to the company's business objectives and client relationships. Stagen trains leaders who are committed to long-term personal development and who seek to use their organizational platforms for positive impact. It offers training programs designed to expand a leader's capacity for wisdom, compassion, and courage. "We want people who think in decades, not years," says Rand. By design, Stagen is a reincarnation of the world's first academy—founded nearly twenty-five hundred years ago by Plato with the goal of self-enlightenment—except here you won't find any toga-clad philosophers or soaring granite columns. (The feta salad is about as Greek as it gets.)

But just in case you're thinking that this academy is home for new-age hippies or transcendentalists, check the client roster. It's filled with C-suite executives and managers at midsize companies with upward of one thousand employees and $50–$500 million in annual revenue. The list is impressive, spanning a wide range of industries and businesses. Stagen only admits the top brass into its ranks because it believes that a company is defined by the people who lead it. "Leaders get the companies they deserve," says Rand, settling into a bean-shaped chair in the tranquil Apollo room. "In the end, organizations are just expressions of their leaders."

This is why Stagen relies on a training strategy that is remarkably direct: If you want to change a company, first improve the leader. To do that, the company created its flagship Integral Leadership Program (ILP), a year-long learning intensive that weaves together in-person workshops, self-directed modules, peer support, phone-based teleclasses, and one-on-one executive coaching. The goal is to change the company from within, starting at the top.

Currently, the academy supports nearly one hundred students in the ILP— their black-and-white headshots hang prominently in the foyer—and counts more than a thousand lifetime members going back to 2001. Stagen provides ongoing study and engagement opportunities for its ILP alumni throughout the year to deepen their mastery of foundational concepts. During my visit, the Athena conference room is in full swing, with members scribbling ways to leverage intangibles on giant whiteboards, something that might have made more sense to me had I not majored in English literature. (Or passed high school algebra.)

There's a good reason corporate leaders sign on to Stagen's year-long program. The curriculum speaks the language of business, with trainings focused on improving attention management, execution, productivity, high-performance teamwork, and other development drivers. For a results-oriented clientele, Stagen delivers a strong product aimed at leaders working in and on their businesses. They also know how to indulge their members. Recruitment events are held at posh hotels and cater to high-end tastes. Aside from its in-house team of trainers and facilitators, the company brings in recognized thought leaders and experts to sharpen best practices. The business-first approach is how Stagen grabs a seat at the table.

But the end game isn't just about creating personal value for leaders. It's about creating *shared values* for organizations. As a company, Stagen believes that business has a higher purpose and, to that end, actively nurtures its academy members to become more conscious, intentional, and process-driven in their leader roles. These soft skills may not be the most visible part of Stagen's offerings, but they're certainly the most sacred.

At one point, Rand leans over and, with hushed fervor, declares, "It's our Trojan horse strategy." Like the mythical gift from Troy whose true purpose remained hidden in plain sight, Stagen's core mission—to create corporate consciousness over the long term—slips in behind a top layer of traditional executive education and consulting. Once leaders get hooked on the practices of operational management, Stagen reels them in with principles of conscious leadership—or, as Rand puts it, "the things that move them from success to significance." For values-driven organizations, that is where the real work begins.

CONSUMERS GETS CONSCIOUS

If you graduated from business school before the Great Recession, the chances that you studied anything having to do with "consciousness" are probably slim. Traditional MBA programs typically dished out meaty helpings of finance, data analytics, microeconomics, and operations—the core of business education. The rest of it was just soft serve, too mushy for a field that loves numbers and data. But that was before the market crashed in 2008 and simmering mistrust of Wall Street finally boiled over. In its wake, people came to believe that business was rigged and corrupt, run over by its own pursuit of profit. Consumers started to care less about a company's size or scale. They wanted to know about its soul.

Around the same time, business began to feel the full brunt of the tech revolution. Not only do today's consumers have greater access to information, but the velocity of innovation and automation is also moving at breakneck speed. Back in the days of industrialization, it could take days, even weeks, to complete jobs or fill orders. Now it's happening in real time. The making and delivery of things is cheaper, quicker, and more complex than at any other point in human history.

Part of that is a natural response to the rise of "applification." People who shop using apps on their phones tend to make smaller purchases in short bursts throughout the day, meaning they're less discerning and more trigger-happy than those who buy from their computers in one sitting or actually walk the aisles. According to eMarketer, mobile shoppers spend more than three times longer using apps than surfing the web. Since the amount of time between wanting and having an item has become ridiculously short—practically nonexistent, if you automate your online cart—buying something requires about as much thought and intent as blinking.

It's also about math. With more connected mobile devices than actual human beings on Earth—7.2 billion and climbing—there is a relentless pressure to make the mobile experience even more attractive, like suggesting the right products or pushing special offers directly to our phones. As mobile drives demand, shoppers have become more finicky, bouncing from deal to deal, scouring the best products. But at the same time, they are demonstrating greater loyalty to the retailers that make them happy. While this kind of soft commitment has posed headaches for sellers, it's also presented them with new opportunities for breaking away from the pack. One way to crawl into the consumer's space is by highlighting values and purpose. Businesses that stand for more than just a product can stand out from their competitors.

And the face of work is changing, too. Millennial workers, who by 2020 will make up nearly half of the American workforce, aren't impressed by legacy structures or leadership siloes. They've come of age during a time when we're laying miles of high-speed fiber optic cable instead of iron railroad ties. As we saw back in chapter 2, companies like Deloitte are putting even more emphasis on developing talent in a way that Regenerates itself. It's safe to say that the twentieth-century focus on process and product has been replaced, maybe irreversibly, by a twenty-first-century outlook on people and purpose. People want more from work than work itself.

So there you have it: public demand for corporate integrity, rapid production cycles, the rise of apps and mobile technology, and an emerging values-driven workforce—that is the state of business today. There is now an opening and appetite for more consciousness in the workplace, meaning that successful companies must pay as much attention to their higher purpose as to their bottom line. That message starts at the top, with the company's leadership. Conscious leaders are moved by meaning and mission, not just power and money. They lead by mentoring, motivating, developing, and inspiring people in a way that shuns command and control. They treat stakeholders as integral company parts, like interlocking gears that turn together. Rather than fuss over how they're going to make it, conscious leaders dream about how they're going to make it *better*.

But to tap that kind of altruism, those at the helm need to shift their focus from being good leaders to becoming good servants. They must perceive a responsibility to serve the purpose of the organization, to support the people within the organization, and to create value for all the organization's stakeholders, not just its investors. Becoming a conscious leader requires thinking in the plural—from "me" to "we"—as well as a passion for addressing nobler issues, like how to create wealth without destroying principles, how to manage with social and environmental responsibility, and what it takes to turn personal gain into global significance. That's certainly a large part of Stagen's mission. But it's also part of a larger movement: Conscious Capitalism.

Founded in 2007, Conscious Capitalism is an organization based around the idea that business is inherently good. With near-evangelical fervor, its members tout free markets and capitalism as the most powerful systems for social cooperation and human progress ever conceived, lifting more people out of poverty and bringing about more prosperity and progress than any other institution in history. As a movement, Conscious Capitalism has called for business to repurpose itself as a global force for social cooperation by acting with greater ethical consciousness.

To do that, businesses that subscribe to the values of Conscious Capitalism follow these four principles:

- They have a higher purpose (*beyond profit*).
- They create and maintain value for all their stakeholders (*not just their investors*).
- They are run by leaders whose mission is to serve and support the company's culture and people (*not simply increase their personal net worth*).
- They create a culture of trust and care between the company and its stakeholders (*not fear and control*).

If you doubt that the pursuit of purpose and profit can coexist, then consider this: Purpose-driven businesses actually outperformed the S&P 500 Index by a factor of fourteen over a fifteen-year period. These companies, affably called "firms of endearment" by Conscious Capitalism cofounder Raj Sisodia, are based on characteristics such as their stated purpose, generosity of compensation, quality of customer service, investment in their communities, and impact on the environment. In other words, they are doing well by doing good.

These are not granola outfits. They are global enterprises whose presence and products are woven into our everyday lives, businesses like 3M (whose creative flair was chronicled in chapter 3), Adobe, Starbucks, T. Rowe Price, Amazon, and Costco. On their way to skyrocketing valuations, these companies are kicking to the curb the idea that big business can't be big hearted. They're also showing what feedforward can accomplish on a company-wide scale. As Bill George, the former CEO of Medtronic, puts it, "Well-run, values-centered businesses can contribute to humankind in more tangible ways than any other organization in society."

Changing from feedback to feedforward can redirect the behaviors of organizations and unlock their higher purpose, but only once we understand the science and psychology of teams. Let's dig in.

COMMUNICATING ACROSS TEAMS

In the last chapter, we looked at what it takes to develop an "inside game." Feedforward guides us to look inward and read the cues that ultimately produce a more intuitive, self-directed plan of improvement. And while it's exhilarating to find and follow our own voice, there's an obvious downside: Self-tuning is great for individuals trying to elevate their performance, but not so great for teams looking to define their purpose.

Here's why: Teams don't live in solitary confinement. They occupy a shared space. So when members of a team become too insular, withdrawing into a state of total introspection, they keep each other at bay. Work stalls. Progress is interrupted. Unless they communicate openly, engage in meaningful give-and-take, and talk through issues, teams will inevitably flame out. They cannibalize themselves through silence.

Once teams develop high levels of communication, they end up with strong bonds of connection. And that allows them to be more than just efficient task completers. It turns them into extraordinary culture creators, the places where larger identities are born. But here's the stubborn thing about culture: It can't be scheduled. It's never coordinated. Rather, the thing we call culture is being shaped all the time, often without us even knowing it.

Take the way we're constantly bumping up against each other at work. We mingle in the hallways, huddle around the coffee machine, and scrunch inside the elevator. The same goes for the encounters we have with members of our own family, who, when you think about it, are just the colleagues we take home with us at the end of the day. We might not love our teams, but we're unavoidably stuck with them at work and at home—whether it's working alongside them on a project or sharing the backseat with them during the morning commute to school.

Every day, our paths inevitably collide. And when they do, we release a running stream of micro-messages in the direction of team members—small signals that let them know what we're thinking or feeling, wanting or needing, loving or hating. At times, the messages are subtle. Other times, not as much. But they're happening *all* the time. And they're one of the most devastating, if silent, forms of feedback that we share.

Micro-messages eventually settle into the big behavioral patterns we know as culture. Culture can be positive. Culture can be poisonous. But whatever form it takes, culture isn't accidental. It grows out of the micro-messages that get passed from person to person, unit to unit, until finally it emerges, unde-clared. Eventually, there is an unofficial but universal acceptance of behaviors and beliefs. And that is the result of a feedback process whose effect on teams cannot be denied.

It doesn't matter whether the "team" is housed inside an office or a classroom or even around the kitchen table. At a certain point, these micro-messages take on a life of their own. If the micro-messages passed around a real estate group communicate failure, then that unit is going to adopt the narrative and never chase the big leads. If the micro-messages spread by teachers stir up grumbling and pessimism, then that faculty is going to adopt the narrative and sink further into toxicity. And if the micro-messages in a household are full of nagging, frustration, and blame, then that family is go-ing to adopt the narrative and spiral into dysfunction.

Now imagine those micro-messages with a future-sounding tone. Instead of reporting negative moments from the past, we'd reframe them with a posi-tive focus on the future. We'd tell each other that we're perfectly capable of landing that deal, jelling as a faculty, or bonding as a family. We would start talking about new possibilities and not let the past define us. Feedforward doesn't just enable individuals to become more creative or conscious. It in-spires teams to think about their passion and purpose. Because when micro-messages crisscross within teams, one of two things happen:

We influence others.

Others influence us.

Two possibilities. That's it.

Regardless of whether we're on the giving or receiving end, the impact of feedforward within teams is remarkable. It may start out unspoken, but its effects are heard loudly across organizations. It's how values are set, decisions are made, and priorities are ordered. And it just so happens to be an inescap-able part of who we are.

HARDWIRED FOR CONNECTION

While we spend much of our childhood practicing social skills, evolution gives us a pretty good head start. Our brains are uniquely designed to read other people's cues and adjust to their perspectives. That's what keeps us from talking too loudly at a dinner party or standing too close to the person in front of us at the checkout line. All this adapting means that we're rarely in a fixed social state. Actually, our social dynamics are rather fluid, moving with the currents of the moment. Based on the information that hits our dashboards, we are constantly shuffling our neurological decks, transmitting and absorbing social cues in real time. For many of us, it happens naturally, almost effortlessly.

To understand why, we need to travel deep inside the mind itself. Just above the brain stem, near the pituitary gland, lies the hypothalamus, an almond-sized region of the brain that links the endocrine and central nervous systems. Anatomically, it is the gatekeeper for much of the body's activities—regulating everything from heart rate and blood pressure to appetite and sleep cycles. By releasing hormones that cause other hormones to either start or stop production, the hypothalamus is the body's version of a household thermostat, taking periodic readings of hormonal settings and deciding whether things need to be adjusted or held in check.

It's here that the body produces a crucial hormone called oxytocin. You've probably heard of it under its better-known trade name Pitocin, a handy drug used to induce labor and help new mothers with lactation. But oxytocin does more than just assist the earliest stages of life. It actually plays a significant role in what happens to us long after we're out of the womb and all grown up.

Oxytocin is one of the most powerful determinants of social behavior. It is the neurobiological element that allows us to read and process social cues—to tell the difference, for instance, between a smile and a smirk or when someone is laughing with us or at us. The higher our oxytocin levels, the better our ability to interpret these social signals.

Scientists have also found that oxytocin relaxes our social inhibition by decreasing anxiety and reducing stress. It diminishes our perceptions of social threats that deter us from engaging with larger groups of people. Most important, oxytocin's release cycle is self-sustaining: The more of it we enjoy, the more willing we are to seek out others and experience enhanced group trust—leading to still more oxytocin production and an even greater appetite for sociability.

All of this is important because it keeps us in constant want of other people's company. The more time we spend with others, the greater the odds that we'll be involved in a group give-and-take, making goal-focused communication like feedback a natural and essentially unavoidable part of our social experiences, wherever they take place. The signal swapping is happening anytime we huddle with colleagues for a strategy session, fret with our kids about a homework assignment, or shoot the breeze with friends over drinks. It affects the way we view events elapsing in real time and possibly even more. In addition to revealing what we see now, our interactions may very well determine what we do *next*.

Brain researchers have long understood the connection between doing and thinking. For every action we take, there's a motor imprint that's left behind. This mental markup helps us replicate the same action again and again. That's why the motor system is so important—it lets us travel from thought to deed in fractions of a second. These neurons fire whether we're repeating a motion or doing it for the first time. Our motor memory makes any act of movement—like typing these very words on my computer—so quick and seamless, we forget it once had to be learned.

But it turns out that neurons don't just light up when we do an action ourselves. They go off when we see that same action performed by *someone else*. These so-called mirror neurons—named for the way the brain mirrors the movements it sees—fire whenever we catch a glimpse of another person doing the things we've done before. Amazingly, just watching others do something has the same cognitive effect as doing it ourselves, even if we fail to lift a finger.

The discovery of mirror neurons was groundbreaking—and, as luck would have it, a rather fortunate accident. Back in the 1980s, a group of brain researchers were studying the motor system of monkeys in Parma, the charming Italian city known for its prosciutto and picturesque countryside views. Inside a university lab, they stashed a pile of peanuts along the rim of a monkey cage and watched the primates go to town. Every time a monkey attempted to take a peanut using a small pincer grasp, a connected brain scanner would crackle to show traces of neural activity. After several days and a few bags of peanuts, not much had happened. The motor system was working as it should.

But then something unexpected occurred. Maybe the monkeys had eaten enough peanuts for one day. Or maybe they were just tired. But at that moment, the monkeys were sitting idly in their cage when one of the researchers, hungry for a snack, reached for some peanuts using the same pincer grasp. Then he heard it—the unmistakable crackle from the scanner. The scientist looked up at the monkeys, who were completely still, then back at the scanner. He took another peanut. Then another. The scanner purred with each attempt. It was picking up signs of motor activity in the monkey's brains, even though they hadn't budged. It didn't seem to matter that no actual movement had occurred. Their brains were mirroring what they were seeing.

And it isn't limited to monkeys. Scientists have discovered that a similar mirror system exists in humans as well. It starts in infancy, when babies mimic the facial expressions of their caregivers, and continues throughout adulthood, when the visuals get more visceral. We erupt after seeing our team hit a game-winning shot, stare in wonder at the antics of street performers, and cry along with the actors who mesmerize us on screen. Mirror neurons let us connect with others, even if it's just by way of observation. They are the living proof of our human craving for socialization. As Robert Krulwich marvels, "Deep in our architecture, down in our cells, we are built to be together."

SHOWING VERSUS SAYING

The science of socialization has major implications for the feedforward we share in teams. The same mirroring that allows infants to copy the expressions of caregivers is also present in organizations, just on a larger and more dynamic scale. Because we're constantly reading and absorbing social cues, we take in these messages all the time and with fairly immediate results—especially if they come from someone with a good view of our work and performance. Nothing new there.

But here's the surprising part: When it comes to giving feedback, the manner drives the message. Or, to put it a bit differently, what we *show* matters more than what we *say*.

That's what researchers found when they studied the impact of feedback given by leaders to their direct reports based on social cues. When critical feedback was expressed with inviting body language—such as smiles and nods—it left a surprisingly happy mark on the moods of the recipients. It turned out that framing a tough piece of news with a positive facial expression softened the blow, making the total picture seem a lot rosier. A simple tweak in affect changed the overall trajectory of the feedback, from bad to better.

The converse held just as true. When positive feedback was delivered with negative cues—like a scowl or frown—it was perceived on the other end to sound critical and unsupportive. People filtered what they heard with a sense of disappointment and failure, even though the actual words being spoken were complimentary. The sunny message got completely wiped out by the sullen manner.

Even more telling, researchers found that the effects of negative social cueing ended up landing harder and lasting longer. While it's natural to remember bad performance reviews from bosses or critical comments from friends, the residual impact is stronger when visual cues are used. In the same study, employees who were treated to positive reviews with scowls and frowns recalled these feedback encounters more intensely and in greater detail than those who received a brighter version of the bad news. Sticking a sad face on feedback apparently made it harder to swallow and, as a result, a lot more memorable.

It comes down to a basic truth about communication: The mind believes what the eye sees. When people are talking to us, our brains are scanning their faces for tell-tale signs—something that lets us know what they *really* believe. A wince, perhaps, or maybe pursed lips. The slant of their eyes. The face is like a storefront that shows a glimpse of the interior goods. It offers public clues about private thoughts. Because our faces reflect our true feelings, most of us helplessly reveal ourselves long before we finish speaking.

Tipping someone off with our facial cues happens so naturally, in fact, that it's evolved into common expressions. We use it to describe people who manage to put on a "brave face," maintain their composure with a "straight face," or act so deceitfully they are nothing but "two-faced." (Interestingly, the Hebrew words for *face* and *inner self* are spelled identically, itself a sign of the face-feeling connection.) Unless you're talking to someone with a "poker face," it's plain to see what's simmering beneath the surface just by looking.

If we see a worrisome sign, we stop listening and start panicking. Could there be something more, something worse, that's about to come out? Recall from chapter 1 that the anticipation of bad news actually shuts down the parts of the brain that allow us to take in and process information. It causes us to temporarily slip into a state of mental paralysis. Once impaired, our fields of view are so constricted that it's hard to tell the difference between what others have said and what we *thought* they said. By the time our brains recover, any positive intent ends up lying in a heap of perceived negativity. Their body language told another story—the one we thought we saw and ultimately came to accept.

Let's bring this concept into focus. Imagine a supervisor pulls you aside and praises you for the report you just prepared. The compliment is nice, but what really stands out is the way her face brightens up, eyes big and expressive, as she tells you how well it was received by the client. You make a point of saying that it couldn't have happened without the help of your two closest team members, whom you immediately tell, in full detail, as soon as the conversation is over. They get visibly excited, too, and the energy bounces around later that day when your group gets together with another team from the same department. And you know why?

Because that's what we're hardwired to do.

Even without putting moods to words, we communicate feelings through the mirroring discussed earlier. We pick up on other people's micro-messages and make them our own. What starts off as a singular feeling quickly turns into a shared view, then a sticky trend, and, finally, an accepted belief.

For many people, being social is pleasurably rewarding: The more of it they enjoy, the more of it they want to experience. That leads to more social contact, and with it, enhanced team trust. Along the way, it produces a kind of social alchemy that keeps connection levels high and performance levels even higher. Simply put, we do our best when we feel our best. And getting others to feel their best starts with a visible signal, not a sound.

CONNECTION LEADS TO CONTRIBUTION

This phenomenon plays out across teams of all types. A principal who puts out a positive vibe while talking to a few teachers in the hallway may discover that the energy spreads to the faculty lounge by lunchtime. Parents who share feedforward with one child—more on that in the next chapter—may realize that siblings start to pick up on the same cues. What we say to one person rarely stays there for long. Before we know it, the message is forwarded to others, affecting their behavior in deep and transformative ways.

This kind of impact doesn't require a grand gesture. It can be something unassuming and simple. Take laughter. You probably didn't realize it at the time, but the laugh you may have shared recently with a colleague or friend was a form of feedback. Those happy peals conveyed a sense of togetherness and created a sense of emotional safety. We don't laugh with the people we don't trust. By laughing with others, we signal that we like them, trust them, and want to share with them. They are worthy of experiencing a piece of our joy.

Good leaders get this. Based on studies of emotional intelligence, some of the top-performing leaders are twice as likely to elicit laughter from their subordinates as their less successful counterparts. From the neuroscience we've combed so far, this makes perfect sense. When subordinates see that the leader is happy, they'll mirror these emotions in their own interactions with others, who in turn do the same. The positivity is multiplied again and again. Sparked by a single person, it grows and spreads to countless others.

But here's the really interesting part: Not only do emotionally savvy leaders create more happiness, but they also increase productivity. They get more out of the people around them. The easy explanation is that people tend to work better when they feel safer. When there's laughter around the workplace, people lower their guard and raise their game. The lightness of the environment makes people less edgy and self-conscious, which sets the conditions for more daring and creative work. Remember the wafer-eating students and inspired companies from chapter 3? There's safety in knowing that we get to live in a future we can control, not a past we can't.

But there's more to it than that. As Rand Stagen showed us at the beginning of the chapter, leaders with long-term outlooks get the people around them to consciously connect to larger causes, and in the process, to one another. That's how organizations and teams come together to produce high-value, long-lasting results. The real thread that joins people together isn't just safety. It's significance—a sense that you belong to something larger than yourself.

That's why laughter is so potent. It may not seem like much, but laughter is the ringtone of inclusion. It's a sign of people connecting on a deep level. Laughter is the sort of thing that continues to compound even as it's spent. By finding ways to laugh with their team, leaders build social capital and trust. It causes people to feel a primal connection to the group and self-identify with its movements, the way ancient tribes used to form around hunting and gathering. In time, as the bonds grow stronger, people start counting their success in team wins, not personal victories. And because people perceive significance in their work, they look for ways to strengthen their social bonds by delivering the best version of themselves, every day.

They maintain connection through contribution.

When that connection is lost or when people feel like they don't belong, the distance puts a freeze on our performance—literally. Researchers have identified a strong link between social exclusion and the perception of coldness. When we meet people who immediately make us feel wanted and connected, we think of them as "warm." But our social thermometers run in both directions, hot *and* cold. Even trivial instances of ostracism—like sensing that we've been snubbed by someone passing us in the hall or in an elevator—can change our perceptions of temperature and send a chill through our interactions.

Ever had a social encounter that wasn't particularly friendly? You'd probably describe the unkind people there as "cold," but it's actually *you* who felt that way. In two studies recalling exclusion, individuals who felt ignored perceived the room as colder than it really was. Not only that, but, in some cases, individuals who felt excluded actually experienced a momentary dip in body temperature and asked for a hot beverage! Sensing that they weren't a part of something, these people felt iced out.

When you put this all together, the feedback we share across teams carries some pretty high stakes for the way others perceive their performance, their sense of purpose, and even their own body temperatures. So what can we do to spread the right kind of messages that leave people feeling empowered, not emptied? The nearby table lists just a few suggestions for connecting more effectively with office colleagues, educators, and even our own children based on three drivers of positive, team-based feedforward.

If there's anything to be learned from the research on laughter, it's that we can't really disentangle how we feel from how we perform. That primal sense of belonging is what supercharges teams or saps their energy. Feedforward allows us to visibly demonstrate—through expressions, not just words—how we feel about others and their significance in our lives. But if the micromessages we project cause more distance than attachment, then all we're doing is leaving people out in the cold.

POSITIVE DRIVERS OF TEAM-BASED FEEDFORWARD	APPLICATIONS		
	IN THE OFFICE	AT SCHOOL	WITH YOUR KIDS
We're hardwired to be social (oxytocin).	Create common areas that allow for casual encounters between coworkers.	Incorporate group learning activities that emphasize discussion and interaction.	Give delicate feedback during a shared family game, activity, or outing.
What we show matters more than what we say.	Relax your facial muscles before talking to one of your reports.	Avoid fidgety behaviors when debriefing teachers after a classroom observation.	Never give feedback in the heat of anger. Hold yourself to a cooling-down period.
Connection leads to contribution.	Plan an after-work social event that's strictly fun.	Create a "get to know you" mixer event for new and veteran teachers.	Turn chores into family affairs—choosing, doing, and rotating household jobs within the family.

GETTING TEAMS TO WORK

So far, we've focused on the underlying cognitive and social factors that impact the way feedforward spreads across teams. But while that's happening in the background, there are several front-end strategies and solutions that can make an immediate difference not only in how teams are designed but also in how feedback within teams is delivered.

1 Size Matters, But So Does Scope

There's plenty of debate about whether big teams create more efficiency or collapse under their own weight. On the one hand, working in a large group can lead to diminished individual effort, or what psychologists have called *social loafing*. The tendency of individuals to become increasingly less productive as the size of their group increases was first noticed in 1913 by French engineer Max Ringelmann, whose famous rope-pulling experiment showed that individuals pulled harder alone than they did as a group. Like the men on the ropes, if we think that someone else will step forward, we feel like we can pull back. There's someone else standing by to pick up the slack. (Remember your last group project?)

More recent studies on the inverse relationship between team size and individual performance point to something called *relational loss*. As the size of a team grows, individual members sense a loss in the support and resources available to them and become discouraged, leading to diminished productivity and work outcomes. When credit and blame are harder to assign, workers may feel disconnected from their jobs. This might be summed up best by the "two pizza" rule of Amazon CEO Jeff Bezos, which holds that if the group needs more than two pizzas for lunch, it's too big.

But while there's compelling evidence to keep teams smaller, it's important to consider the scope of their work. Big teams can deliver big results, especially for challenging tasks. One prominent study found that for complex problem-solving tasks, groups of three, four, or even five people working together performed better than an equivalent number of superior individuals working alone. According to researchers, the team advantage arises from people working together to generate and adopt correct responses, reject erroneous possibilities, and effectively process information. In other words, the feedback shared among the group became its secret weapon.

So if you're trying to build a team, take note of the task. Managers should beef up teams during early stage research and development, when sophisticated engineering solutions are needed, but slim them down during late-round product delivery, when the need for speed and agility takes over. Teachers should consider grouping students together for complex problem-solving activities that require deep analysis rather than those that only need rote memorization. And it may be more advantageous to assemble a small committee to plan the neighborhood July 4 picnic but a large advisory to develop the city highway-renovation project. Whether feedback proves to be a team's asset or Achilles' heel may have more to do with the scope of the problem, not the size of the team.

2 Agree to Disagree

We commit enormous energy and resources to designing highly agreeable teams, thinking that harmony is key to their success. How many times have we hesitated to turn something over to a group of people plagued by conflict? Well, it turns out our fears may be unfounded. New research shows that a healthy amount of disagreement within a team might actually be a good thing. Even if team members can't agree on a final answer, the process of consensus building can prove valuable in the long run.

That's what researchers discovered when they invited pairs of eight-year-old students to predict whether an empty metal box or solid rubber ring would float in water. As you might expect with young children, there was strenuous debate among some of the partners about the answer, for reasons that may or may not have had anything to do with density or buoyancy. Once pairs agreed on a prediction, they tested it and moved on.

A few weeks later during a final assessment, students were asked to show their knowledge of what happened during the experiment. The pairs that engaged in more back-and-forth debate showed better delayed post-test results than those who had reached immediate consensus. Even though they couldn't settle right away on an answer, the pairs that had to grind their way to agreement were forced to clarify their assumptions and strengthen their understanding of the lesson in ways the others did not.

We may be taught from a young age that it's not polite to argue, but that doesn't mean it can't be beneficial. Back in chapter 2, we saw how the team that vigorously debated ways to reduce Bay Area traffic ended up with better and longer-lasting ideas than more mild-mannered planners. They showed that feedforward Expands the way people think by inviting just enough discomfort to make things more interesting.

3 Safety First

But for all the constructive benefits, there is a downside to speaking up: fear. When we sense potential conflict with the people seated around the table, our guard goes up. Way up. We begin to wonder: *How is this going to play? Are people going to think I'm crazy or stupid for saying this?* Until we can tell whether our words will be vilified or validated by the people seated around the table, silence becomes our best self-defense. That means that some of the best ideas may never get airtime simply because we're too afraid to watch them get mercilessly beaten down.

For many, leaping into the unknown won't happen unless they jump with an emotional parachute, or what scientists call "psychological safety." Amy Edmonson of Harvard Business School defines this as "a sense of confidence that the team will not embarrass, reject or punish someone for speaking up." It emerges from a shared belief among members of a team that it's safe to go out on a limb and do some interpersonal risk taking. Others may not agree with what we have to say, but at least we know they won't ridicule us for saying it. As we saw a few pages earlier with the laughter studies, people need to know that it's safe to step beyond their comfort zones.

Psychological safety is a powerful force in the way teams behave, and it might well play a key role in how they perform. That's what Google found when the company started gathering data on itself to see what made its best teams tick. Code-named Project Aristotle, the internal study of 180 functional teams aimed to uncover why some groups succeeded while others stumbled. If it could find the master gene, Google could clone all its teams around it.

After a series of trials, Google's research analysts failed to turn up a reliably consistent pattern of high performance—what worked for one team differed sharply from another—until the researchers used psychological safety as the litmus. Finally, the fog lifted and a clearer picture of team excellence emerged. What seemed to count the most was not some fancy metric but a fundamental norm: the ability of group members to think and act without worrying about social repercussions—basically, to just be themselves.

There's a broader implication here for sharing feedforward as well. When people go to work, they bring their whole selves to the endeavor. That includes all the baggage and burdens they carry with them from home to work and back. A concern about a sick child. A home repair gone awry. By acknowledging another person's concerns, be they work-related or not, organizations create a culture of trust and care, the fourth pillar of Conscious Capitalism and an otherwise sensible leadership practice regardless of a company's stated mission and goals. Letting people know that it's okay to speak up creates the psychological safety that is missing in too many work environments today.

■ ■ ■

Back at Stagen, there's a peculiar picture that visitors pass on their way in and out of the academy. It's a map of the London Underground, the complex network of transit lines, stops, and services that connect one of the world's busiest cities. The map was designed in 1931 by an Englishman named Harry Beck, an engineering draftsman who drew up the map while working for the London Underground Signals Office. Beck wasn't the first person to create a visual rendition of the Underground—there had been several other maps in circulation since the early 1920s—but his diagram became an immediate hit, with public demand for the new design surpassing seven hundred thousand copies. Beck's secret? Simplicity.

Rather than laying out different transit lines geographically, with routes superimposed over a city grid, Beck created a scaled-down map that showed the relative positions of the stations, lines, and fare zones. Colored lines and easy-to-spot symbols gave Tube riders an immediate view of where they were and needed to go. Beck had a hunch that commuters were more interested in getting from point A to point B than knowing the actual distance between them. He was right. His proportional design has been copied by map makers ever since, from universities and hospitals to museums and zoos.

Easy to navigate. Highly usable. Simple.

Rand Stagen studies the picture. "This is exactly what we're doing," he says, tracing imaginary lines across the map. "Our job is to help leaders stay on purpose while navigating the complexities of their organizations and markets." He pauses. "We give them the maps to do that." The map is a metaphor for the work of Stagen in particular and the Conscious Capitalism movement as a whole. Getting to where you're going means taking a long view of the

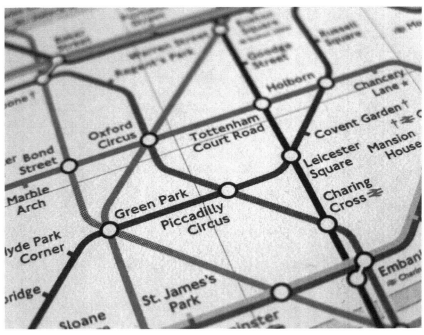

Source: Thinkstock Images. *Credit:* Claudio Divizia

journey, noticing the landmarks that bring you closer to the destination, and recognizing that sooner or later all roads intersect. It's as true of conscious leadership as it is of commuter lines. In the end, we're inescapably connected to what's around us.

It also shows why feedforward can be a powerful accelerant for teams. In an age when we're more hyperconnected than ever, what we say or show to one person rarely stays there for long. Feedback ripples through the everyday interactions we have with coworkers and colleagues, family and friends. It passes through the social cues we see and the laughter we share. And it can help different people on the same team form unusually deep connections, leading to better work, stronger bonds, and all-around emotional safety.

Some of that comes from a neurological drive to be social but even more so from a spiritual need to be significant—to stretch for something larger than ourselves. But before people can rise to that challenge, they have to be able to stand on their own. Done well, feedforward helps upgrade our capacity for independence. All around us, people are searching for the confidence and competence to take control of their own lives. The next chapter shows them how.

6

Autonomy

For the record, Yolanda Mendoza had done her homework. But as the teacher walked around the room collecting assignments, Yolanda bowed her head, empty handed. Like the rest of her things, it was at home, tucked inside the backpack that got left behind in the morning rush. It's not uncommon for kids to forget their stuff, and for all kinds of reasons—they're scatterbrained, slow movers, or chronically late for the bus. But Yolanda was a pretty responsible kid and normally didn't have to hustle. On this particular morning, she wasn't running toward something. She was running *from* it.

Her father, an alcoholic, had just returned home after an especially hard night of drinking, the sharp smell of tequila trailing close behind. In their neighborhood of Guelavia, a small town of about three thousand in the southwest highlands of Oaxaca, locals knew him for his cold demeanor and hot temper. To this day, Yolanda can't remember what sent her father flying into a violent rage, but she and her seven siblings knew the signs. They had to get out of the house, and fast. The backpack was a distant afterthought.

"It was hard for me to stay focused in class," remembers Yolanda, now in her thirties. "I was always worried that my mother was being beaten at home while I was in school." Besides living under the specter of abuse, Yolanda also faced a language barrier. She was brought up with Zapoteco, a dialect spoken by Mexico's indigenous Zapotec community. Traditional Spanish was so foreign that she could barely participate in classroom activities. Her mother wasn't much help at home, either. But with determination and the extraordinary support of one of her teachers, Yolanda eventually mastered the language and earned a top rank in her class by the time she completed middle school.

Things continued to look up from there. When she turned eighteen, Yolanda moved with her mother and siblings to California, where she settled in with a family as their full-time babysitter. When the family relocated to Hawaii, Yolanda decided to go with them, which ended up being a smart move: Not long after that, she met her future husband, Rudy, a soft-spoken irrigation technician from Monterrey. After a few more years by the beach, the couple decided they'd had enough of sand and shore, and in 2006 they moved to Dallas, where they started a family of their own. For a short time, it looked like Yolanda's life, so full of fear and pain, had turned a corner.

But the dark shadows of her past continued to linger. "As a parent, you do the same things you saw your parents do," she says, her bouncy voice trailing off for a moment. "I was always getting angry so quickly, always yelling at my kids, even for the smallest things." She began to feel the invisible grip of her father take hold at home. Tensions ran high, sometimes boiling over. No matter how hard she tried to leave him behind, Yolanda could feel her father catching up with her, opening fresh wounds in her family life. "What I really needed was a place that could show me how to do things differently, how to parent differently."

That place is the Momentous Institute. True to its name, Momentous has a grand plan—to change the odds for some of the neediest children and their families. Operating across two urban campuses in Dallas, Momentous provides educational and therapeutic programs to over six thousand children and family members a year, most of them minorities facing economic hardship. Median household income for families receiving therapy sits below the poverty line at $21,650 a year. Eighty-six percent qualify for free or reduced lunches. And a majority of families live in depressed neighborhoods that are havens of crime, abuse, and neglect. The challenges are real and ever present, which is why the mission of Momentous—to build and repair social and emotional health through education, therapeutic programs, research, and training—has attracted generous support.

The institute was founded nearly a century ago by the Salesmanship Club of Dallas, a service organization of more than six hundred business and community leaders committed to transforming lives. Their signature event—the AT&T Byron Nelson, a championship golf tournament on the PGA Tour—hauls in nearly $6 million a year for the institution.

Powered by the philanthropic efforts of the Salesmanship Club and other donors, Momentous employs a robust mental-health staff of psychologists, intake coordinators, clinicians, case managers, and family educators. Through parenting groups and therapy sessions, social workers and counselors equip families with trauma-informed strategies that strengthen social-emotional health and help them cope more effectively with setbacks.

By all counts, they're making an impact. In 2015, Momentous delivered therapeutic services to more than six thousand children and family members, including parent education and clinical interventions by licensed mental-health professionals. Over the past five years, the total number of unique clients has surpassed twenty-two thousand, an average of about twenty people per day. These are impressive stats, but behind the gaudy numbers lies a simple notion and the institute's guiding belief: The road to better outcomes starts with stronger families.

That line of support runs through the Momentous School, which opened its doors in 1997 as the city's first urban laboratory school attending to the social and emotional health of children. It caps enrollment at 248 students, from pre-K three-year-olds through fifth grade, and keeps classes small—no more than sixteen children per section. Every seat is filled. Some students walk around in khakis and cherry-red polos, others in matching sweatshirts with a collegiate-looking blue letter *M* spread across the front. There's the usual slate of math and reading, plus specialties like music and art—the sort of program you might recognize if you wandered into a fancy private school somewhere in suburbia.

Except it doesn't take long to realize that Momentous is a school with different stripes. For starters, you're just as likely to find parents roaming the halls as kids. After morning drop-off, many of them head over to Momentous's Parent Center, a community meet-up for daily classes ranging from aerobics to crochet, mostly led by the parents themselves. They use the space to chat and catch up on each other's lives. During my visit, a few women were putting the finishing touches on the oil canvases they had begun in a parent art class. Others had just baked and decorated cupcakes for a new mother. In the spring, the room fills with volunteers working on the school's float for the city's annual Cinco de Mayo parade. Even with space inside the building at a premium, the Parent Center remains sacred. It's for parent use only.

And for good reason. Momentous has established a carefully designed plan to take parent engagement to the next level. Here, you won't find room parents or a formal Parent-Teacher Association; they don't exist. Instead, the school invites parents and trusted adults to help serve breakfast and lunch up to twelve times per year. That means that children routinely see their parents, relatives, and neighborhood friends in and around the building throughout the day. At many schools, this kind of pop-in culture would be frowned upon, but at Momentous it's part of the educational philosophy. By choice, the school functions as an extension of the home. Parental presence isn't just welcomed. It's encouraged.

Parental involvement starts right away. When parents enroll their kids for the first time, Momentous asks them to write something it calls vision statements—handwritten one-page letters to their children. It's a chance for parents to telegraph their deepest held beliefs and dreams and to imagine the sort of lives their children might someday lead. The vision statements are clear and poignant, full of heart, hope, and a bit of parental grief. Some look out as far as college and careers. Others focus on more immediate goals, like mastering subtraction and English prepositions. Many talk about God and abiding by one's faith. The words are unsparingly raw and real.

But the most astonishing thing about these vision statements is that they're public. Instead of hiding somewhere in a file cabinet, they hang in plain sight along the back wall of the Parent Center, displayed like a permanent exhibit. The themes they express hit so close to home, you might actually think you're reading about your own child in someone else's letter—proof that when it comes to raising kids, even complete strangers think like kindred spirits. In the end, they just want to give them the best.

Having parents write vision statements is not just symbolic but also tactical. Knowing more about what really matters to parents gives the school's professional staff a keener sense of where they're heading and how to get there. They plot their course of prevention and intervention around it. The families shape the path, while the teachers and therapists clear the trail. Working together, albeit from different angles, both sides try to figure out the best route to get there. Along the way, they teach children to believe that the adults in their lives see promise in their journey.

It's this combination of strong relationships and high expectations that has made Momentous a winning example of urban education. They know it, too, based on years of longitudinal tracking and research. More than seven years after leaving Momentous, a whopping 99 percent of alumni graduate high school on time. Eighty-six percent advance to higher education, and nearly nine in ten college freshmen reenroll for their sophomore year. Compared to national surveys on college attendance, which put the admission rate for low-income students below 50 percent, the people at Momentous aren't just changing the odds. They're crushing them.

But why?

FROM VICTIMS TO CREATORS

Earlier in the book, we showed the power of feedforward that is Particular and Expands. We saw it ignite the imaginations of the creative kids at the Rama School and drive up levels of employee engagement and performance at companies like Deloitte. But there's more to this process than just relinquishing control. If all you're prepared to do is pull back, then the only thing you'll produce is empty space. The secret to letting go isn't what you give up. It's what you *give*.

When we give feedforward and talk to other people about their strengths and burgeoning potential, we hand them the tools of autonomy, or self-management. (The concept originates from the Greek words *autos*, self, and *nomos*, rule.) Communicating this way helps others face setbacks with resilience, disappointment with determination, and adversity with hope. It unlocks what personality psychologists call an internal locus of control, or the belief that every action, good or bad, is controlled by our own efforts. We can't change the hand we're dealt, but we do have a say in how it's played.

Most people don't think about feedback as a way to build autonomy. Actually, they have the totally opposite view: Feedback is how we tell people about the things they *aren't* doing well, how they're *not* managing their roles and responsibilities, and why they *shouldn't* be trusted to take care of themselves. This has the downward effect of turning people into victims, casualties of their own shortcomings. After getting feedback, they feel less capable and empowered, not more. And while that's probably the last thing anyone giving feedback wants to do, it's also the likeliest outcome.

Little wonder, then, that managers and parents alike treat feedback with a mixture of fear and loathing—less intimidating and more enjoyable than getting a root canal, perhaps, but not by much. The tactics of traditional feedback—rooted in the past, focused on the things we can't change—leave people powerless, filled with the same helpless frustration that you'd feel after becoming the victim of identity fraud or theft. The only difference is that instead of taking their property, we use feedback to take their pride. But it doesn't have to be that way.

With feedforward, we direct our feedback toward people's strengths and future prospects, changing feedback's purpose and perception. Traditional feedback ends with finger-pointing and frustration. It turns people into victims. But feedforward climaxes in optimism and opportunity. It turns people into *creators*—the ones who manage to turn challenge into opportunity. That's why the kids at Momentous are so good at beating back the odds. For all the messiness that surrounds them, they don't buy into the victim narrative, choosing instead to fight adversity with action. The people around them give feedforward that breeds resilience and pushes the idea that fate isn't what happens—it's what happens *next*.

But to become a creator, you need tools. And not just the traditional set of cognitive tools that widen our view of the world but also a range of techniques that allow you to make sense of it, even when it's chaotic and unforgiving. And that's exactly where Momentous relentlessly applies its efforts and focus. "In the time of Google, knowledge isn't the differentiator. Social emotional health is," declares Michelle Kinder, the executive director of Momentous. "Kids need to know how to think, not just what to think."

If anyone gets this, it's Kinder. She's been with Momentous for nearly twenty years, first as a family therapist, then running its therapeutic service program, and now leading day-to-day operations and strategy. Tall, with a soothing southern drawl, Kinder can hold court when it comes to the science and sociology of poverty and toxic stress on children. "When kids go into an amygdala hijack, you can't logic them out of their trauma," she says, referring to the part of the brain that processes primal emotions like fear and anger. "You have to first calm them down, and then you can talk about consequences and acceptable behavior and appropriate actions."

Think of the brain like one of those jack-in-the-box toys you played with as a kid. You know there's something hiding inside the box, crouched beneath the lid. For a while, that's where it stays, flat and secured—that is, until the crank gets turned one time too many, releasing the catch on the lid and sending the toy flying up. Similarly, our emotions "pop" just like the weasel: It's only a matter of time before the amygdala's stress-inducing energy causes us to blow our tops and spring those pent-up emotions into action.

But unlike the weasel, we can actually stop the pop before it happens. This is where social-emotional habits play a pivotal role. At Momentous, students learn to live alongside the stress they experience every day. With a strong emphasis on brain-based learning, they become familiar with the inner workings of the central nervous system, right down to the cellular level. Students even make wearable brains with full views of its lobes and stem. (If it weren't so cool, it would be gross.) Knowing what's happening down in the brain's architecture is the first step toward controlling the toxic stress that floods it. Rule number one for creators: If you can name it, you can tame it.

"SETTLE YOUR GLITTER"

The costs of not managing emotional stress are high. As we learn new information, we are constantly generating new neurons in the hippocampus, the part of the brain associated with learning, memory, and emotion. But ongoing stress can halt neuron production and slow the connections between hippocampal cells. The really bad news? It doesn't take much for that to happen. In an animal study, scientists found that possibly just *one* stressful event could destroy newly created neurons in the hippocampus.

Here's why: When we're stressed, the body releases cortisol, a steroid hormone. Elevated cortisol levels can cause a whole lot of harm, like lower immune function, higher blood pressure, increased weight gain, and other ills. These biomarkers aside, there's also good reason to worry about cortisol's effects on learning and emotional regulation, especially in young children.

While cortisol hampers the activity of the hippocampus, it actually *increases* the size and activity of the amygdala, the brain's fear processor. That triggers our threat perception, putting our bodies into "fight or flight" mode. For some adults, that means retreat and submission. For others, it ends in bare-knuckled confrontation. But with kids especially, it can produce an ominous third response: brain freeze.

Think back to what it must have felt like to be Yolanda Mendoza that fateful morning. Her cortisol levels were spiked. Toxic stress flooded her neural pathways, sending her amygdala into a frenzy. Sitting at that desk, fretting about the missing homework, Yolanda was present and absent all at once. Even without her backpack, Yolanda still lugged around a different kind of baggage—unseen, of course, but no less heavy. In a state of heightened threat awareness, Yolanda's traumatized brain was essentially frozen, too impaired for higher-order processing and reasoning tasks. And yet so many teachers, unaware of this invisible toll, relentlessly press kids like her forward, even as toxic stress pulls them back.

What they need is a brain changer. And that's exactly what Momentous tries to deliver, starting with the feedback that's initiated and practiced throughout the day. But it's not what you'd expect. Instead of talking about performance, Momentous focuses on potential—not who students are right now, but who they're *going* to be and what they can do to get there. They deliver feedforward that builds autonomy and speaks to the creator inside of every child.

A big part of that comes by practicing self-regulation. All the brain-based talk around Momentous is more than just show. It's a slice of life, carved into daily learning activities and experiences. One way this happens is through the "brain breaks" that students take multiple times each day.

Starting with its youngest group, the three-year-olds, Momentous gets kids engaged in deep breathing and mindful focus. They close their eyes, fold their hands across their laps, and inhale slowly, their tiny chests rising and falling with each deliberate breath. The breathing provides a rhythm, but it's the mindfulness that makes the magic. They concentrate on the source of conflict, contain it, and tie it off from the outside world. As kids get older, the brain breaks are longer and more frequent. By the time they open their eyes, their world is a calmer, more controlled place.

The secret to self-management, kids learn, is to "settle your glitter." Around Momentous, that's more than just a mantra. It's something students can touch and feel, called glitter balls—small, reddish-looking globes about the size of a plum filled with a solution of water and glitter. (Just don't call it a snow globe. The kids will correct you.) When you shake the glitter ball, its sparkly contents swirl around like a category-four tornado. But when the ball is held still, the glitter starts to sink, settling into clumpy piles along the base.

The lesson is symbolic: When the mind is beset by toxic stress (the glitter), it can't see through the storm and make sense of the surrounding chaos.

That's when our brains are prone to one of those fight-flight-freeze responses. But once we settle the mind and place it into a state of deliberate calm, stress levels recede and become less toxic, yielding an uncluttered view of the world. The stress factors don't magically disappear. They may even stir up again. But for the moment, they're silent and made to rest.

This is what happens when feedforward is geared toward Impact. It makes it possible for people to get out in front of a problem before it runs them over. What makes the glitter ball so powerful isn't the material it contains but the messages it conveys: *You hold your fate in your own hands.* Combined with the vision statements—little pieces of which show up all over the school, from the kids' lockers to classroom doors—what you find is a culture of visible empowerment, a place where adults teach kids to become . . . adults. By helping children develop healthier habits of self-regulation and self-image, Momentous makes it possible for them to meet stress with strength. They develop the will to lead. They become creators, not victims.

Giving people the tools they need to be successful isn't just noble—it's smart practice. A relative of mine lives in Philadelphia, where the winter storms can be particularly brutal, causing frequent electrical outages. After losing power (and the contents of her freezer) for the third time, she decided that enough was enough. She sprang for a standby private generator that keeps her home warm and bright even when the rest of her block is sitting in the dark, maybe wishing they had done the same. When conditions are bad, she doesn't rely on the regional electric provider for power. She generates it herself.

Moving feedback out of the victim column and into the creator column has a similar effect. Feedforward gets people to secure their own success by keeping them powered up even when there's no charge coming from another source. Rather than make feedback about managing, we change the focus to messaging—sharing bits of information that help others realize their own strengths and energy supply. That approach builds capacity, increases attention, curbs uncertainty, and restores confidence. And it's a whole lot cheaper than putting in a thirty-kilowatt home generator.

Feedforward is a useful fix for just about anyone trying to bring out someone else's best. It's true for teachers working with at-risk youth, managers dealing with anxious employees, or parents launching their reluctant children. Remember what we said before: *Letting go isn't what you give up.*

It's what you give. And when you give other people feedback that helps them rise, not fall, then you are providing them with the sure-footedness to stand on their own.

MESSAGES FROM HOME

Looking at Yolanda Mendoza and others like her, it's clear that feedforward can become an autonomy driver. But you also start to notice that a good deal of the grooming starts late, long after time has hardened bad habits. The parenting books, the teacher trainings, the federal programs—they all maintain that intervening early is a crucial step. But how early?

There's good evidence that suggests autonomy-building feedback starts in infancy. Take this scene: It's the middle of the night, and a new mother is awakened by the whimpering of her six-week-old son in the room next door. Fighting sleep, she picks up the child and cradles him in her arms, her eyes locking on his. The cries quickly turn to coos, which draws an even stronger emotional reaction from the mother. He looks up; she looks back. What began as a cry for help morphs into a call of love.

Researchers refer to these face-to-face exchanges as "serve and return" interactions. They work just like they sound: Babies instinctively "serve" up a call for attention—they gurgle, flail their tiny arms and bodies, make adoring facial gestures, and let out piercing screams. In response, caregivers "return" the call with a supportive gesture. They'll nestle the baby in their arms, gaze lovingly into his or her eyes, and, if it's been a few hours, offer a satisfying meal.

There's more to serve and return interactions than just a parent-child volley match. A positive "return" by caregivers shows that they can be counted on to provide attention and support. Even in infancy, children can begin to sense whether their needs will be met reliably and predictably or whether their calls will go unanswered. Responsive relationships enlarge their capacity for trust, play, and eventually love—the comforting sense that someone on the other side is watching, waiting, and willing to return the call.

But what if no one picks up?

When an adult's responses to a child are unreliable, inappropriate, or simply absent, the effects can be devastating. Rather than filling up on positive signs of safety, the developing brain floods with harmful signals of stress, which can impair the still-new and rapidly forming neural connections that determine motor skills, memory, emotion, and behavioral control—the basis for emotional and cognitive functioning later in life. For good or bad, serve and return experiences make a profound impact on who this child is and will one day become.

The molding continues even as kids grow out of infancy and into early childhood. Psychologists, including Mary Dozier at the University of Delaware and Philip Fisher at the University of Oregon, have studied home-visiting interventions in which foster parents of young children receive supportive, personalized coaching to help them sustain high levels of warmth and trust with their kids. The purpose of the home visits isn't to "grade" parents on how well they are managing their roles, but rather to offer encouragement and insights that guide their steps.

As a feedback method, home visits can be highly effective. In one series of experiments, infants and toddlers whose foster parents received just ten home visits showed fewer behavior problems than a control group and reported significantly higher rates of "secure attachment" with the adults in their lives. Their ability to manage stress improved, too. Their cortisol levels, a hormonal indicator of stress, fell more in line with those of typical, well-functioning, non-foster-care children.

With an impact like that, people start to notice. Back at Momentous, home visits are a critical part of the parent engagement process. Before the start of the school year and every month thereafter, family coordinators and therapists drop by the homes of students in the three- and four-year-old classes. They take along clear plastic crates filled with interesting games, toys, and activities and initiate a three-way playdate between them, the parents, and the kids. In some cases, the visiting professional models appropriate use of the toys or puts a creative twist on the activity.

After an hour or so, the home visitor leaves but the crate stays—for nearly two more weeks. That gives families plenty of time to gather as a whole unit and interact with its contents. But the goal is more than just play. As custodians of the crate, participants are asked to journal about their experiences in an accompanying spiral-bound notebook. Nothing too formal—just what they liked, how they used the contents, and any memorable moments they want to share. When the crate is eventually collected and passed on to another family, so is the journal, tying together the reflections of total strangers into one connected feedback narrative.

That's the irony of autonomy: To become truly independent, we need the support of other people. Michelle Kinder, the Momentous director, agrees. "We have to make sure that people feel seen, which is particularly important for families who have felt marginalized or invisible," she says. Surprisingly, even though the families that attend Momentous live within a five-mile radius of the school, many are barely acquaintances. Some have never even met before.

It doesn't take long for that to change. The school arranges "engagement nights" for new families to get to know each other but leaves the planning to them. "The magic comes from releasing the power and allowing the parents to create their own spaces," says Kinder. Over the years, parents have come up with creative themes, from family-style *loteria*, a Spanish variation of bingo, to a gallery walk through a homemade museum showcasing the range of their distinct cultures and backgrounds. Like we said before: *Letting go isn't what you give up. It's what you give.*

The engagement night is the first of many occasions when parents will sense that someone else is standing beside them. And not just the professionals—other people, just like them. Because classes are small and keep their composition from year to year (enrollment changes are rare), families in the same cohort get to know one another intimately during those eight years from preschool to fifth grade. They share milestones together. Many begin to socialize outside of school. Pulled from the shadows of anonymity, these one-time strangers become each other's surrogates and caretakers. That, more than anything else, restores social-emotional health and wholeness in their lives.

There's a reason why this place succeeds in a space where so many do not. Reading the vision statements, seeing the parents amble about, I come to realize that Momentous isn't merely a school for the community. It's a school that *is* a community. And by delivering feedforward to parents and students that is personal, visible, and makes an undeniable Impact, it underscores the value of strengths-based feedback that lifts people out of victimhood. But rising up demands a certain amount of reaching out. The thing about autonomy is that you never find it alone.

THE THREE Ss OF AUTONOMY

So far, we've focused on the change efforts of a single organization with a highly defined clientele. Watching how it all came together makes you wonder: Are there lessons here for others that aren't quite as specialized—like schools with broader service mandates or companies with far-reaching business objectives? Can feedforward that focuses on strengths build autonomy elsewhere, and if so, how?

For that, meet Camille Farrington. A former high school teacher turned researcher, Farrington spent fifteen years toiling in Chicago's inner-city schools. In that time, she began to notice that the biggest contributor to student success had little to do with the usual factors singled out by reformers. It wasn't a student's intelligence or access to outside resources. It didn't depend on the amount of money districts poured into books or teaching materials. And it had surprisingly little to do with the rank or experience of teachers, the tenure of the principal, or the support services that were offered by counselors or academic advisors.

What it boiled down to was something Farrington calls "academic perseverance." This sounds an awful lot like another catch phrase, "grit," which has received considerable attention of late in educational and parenting circles. But unlike grit, which is generally seen as a stable quality, academic perseverance is more fluid, meaning that it varies case by case. It's possible for students to possess academic perseverance when studying fractions but not when they are rewriting an essay. Or for them to demonstrate it while rehearsing a musical piece at school with a tutor but not at home with a parent. If grit is a general reading of who we are *all* the time, then academic perseverance is a measure of who we are at a given *moment* in time. It comes and goes in passing waves.

Thinking about that distinction in practical terms, we might be better off trying to build academic perseverance than attempting to teach grit. Because academic perseverance is bound by variable conditions, not deep-seated human nature, there is a greater chance it can be calibrated and controlled. For her part, Farrington has condensed the bulky literature on noncognitive performance traits into a simpler road map. She thinks that by holding to just four beliefs, students can pummel through adversity to reach lasting success. They are:

1. I belong in this academic community.
2. My ability and competence grow with my effort.
3. I can succeed at this.
4. This work has value for me.

For just a moment, remove the word *academic* from the top of Farrington's list. What you're left with is a fairly universal formula for building autonomy across all fields and disciplines. It's true, of course, that Farrington's work is thinly sliced around the habits of students at school. But its application should extend equally well to employees at work and, for that matter, parents at home. After all, perseverance isn't just required when you're sitting in a classroom. It matters regardless of who or where you are.

So what are the broader lessons of perseverance, and how can feedforward deliver those results? It starts with a few qualities we'll call the three Ss of autonomy: support, sweat, and significance. Let's take a closer look at each one.

1 Support

We got to see how Momentous develops strong relationships with parents and children and helps them regain their footing. But fostering that kind of support is also critical to the workplace, especially when it concerns the onboarding process. Imagine you're an engineer just hired by a multinational manufacturing company. Aside from knowing little, if anything, about your new team's work style, professional history, or internal politics, you're struggling to figure out basic functions, like how to get your hands on a purchase order or where to find a working stapler.

This is where Farrington's first principle—*I belong in this academic community*—enters the fray. Trading the academic community for the business environment, we find that the social bonds so vital to the teacher-student relationship are equally important to the manager-employee dynamic. But here's the crucial difference: Whereas teachers tend to be the chief purveyors of knowledge to students, managers provide significantly fewer inputs, ceding that responsibility to subordinates who work alongside one another.

Researchers found that about 65 percent of what new employees learn comes directly from their coworkers, while only 15 percent traces back to interactions with managers. That puts added weight onto the shoulders of current employees, who end up having to steer newcomers through unfamiliar territory. Onboarding is always difficult, but whether a new hire fits in around the office may come down to more than just political savvy or people skills. It depends on the extent to which colleagues develop high-quality work relationships, make themselves available as mentors, and offer tips about how things get done on the ground.

Russell Korte, the study's lead researcher and an expert on workplace dynamics, advises companies to provide new hires with "local mentors" to show them the ropes and for managers to grab regular face time with newcomers during the first few months after they're hired. All that pervasive feedback—the coaching, priming, and navigating—helps to build the confidence and job capacity of new recruits. The alternative can be damaging not only to the employee but also to the employer. Falling back on a sink-or-swim mentality will ultimately harm organizations and possibly drain them of their best talent.

Creating a soft landing for new hires may also carry performance advantages: In one study, friendship groups—teams that reported a high level of connection both within and beyond their work space—performed better than acquaintance groups on decision-making and motor tasks. All signs pointed to their enhanced level of group commitment and cooperation.

The competitive edge gained by strengthening social bonds explains why the most progressive companies, such as Facebook and Google, provide opportunities for shared games, meals, and exercise and why legacy organizations such as McKinsey and Chevron have built alumni networks that encourage employees to invest in relationships, even if they don't envision sticking around for long. The lesson: To reach the top, you need help from all sides.

2   Sweat

Legendary UCLA men's basketball coach John Wooden once said, "Success travels in the company of very hard work." That couldn't be truer when considering the ways in which people achieve the high mark of success: the ability to perform or complete a task on their own. It brings to mind the second and third principles on Farrington's list: *My ability and competence grow with my effort* and *I can succeed at this.*

The connection between competence and effort has been covered extensively. Most people get that it takes a lot of sweat to succeed. But deep down, there's a part of us that secretly wants, even *prefers*, to see achievement as effortless, something that grows naturally from talent, not over time. That was the conclusion of a recent study showing how a bias for "naturalness" shapes our perceptions of performance. Researchers rounded up hundreds of expert musicians and read them a bio of a solo pianist, played an audio clip of his work, and asked them to rate the musical performance. They then repeated the process for a second pianist. The two pieces sounded nearly identical, except researchers described the first artist as a "natural," someone with innate talent, and the second artist as a "striver," someone with hard-earned achievement. The group of musicians listening to both performances overwhelmingly rated the "natural" more highly than the "striver," which seemed innocent enough, except they had been tricked: These two pianists were, in fact, *just one person*. The same soloist had played both pieces. The group's bias for naturalness betrayed their classically trained ears.

The subtle privileging of talent over effort isn't limited to music. Researchers found a similar phenomenon when it came to entrepreneurship, and there's even evidence that it exists among children and gets stronger as they grow up. "We're likely to say that we value hard work," says Chia-Jung Tsay, the study's author. "But then this apparently hidden preference emerges when we test real behaviors."

The idea that someone can just cruise across the finish line without breaking a sweat is alluring but rarely true. In the end, achievement is about sticking to the steps: setting performance goals, expecting hours of effort, and using feedback to adjust the process. Even naturals do a lot of striving. They understand, as Farrington's list shows, that it takes lots of practice before we find our purpose.

3 **Significance**

But perhaps the most important driver of autonomy is significance: the sense that what we're doing matters to us or to others. We are not motivated solely by the material consequences of our actions but by the intrinsic joy those actions bring us. So when it comes time to perform a task—doing a homework assignment, filing a status report, or volunteering for the homeowner's association—we instinctively weigh its importance on a significance scale: Will doing this action cause heightened or diminished joy to me or to those close to me? Is there some enduring value to the work, or will its completion leave me feeling emptier, not more satisfied?

This calculation happens all the time. And it comes down to a basic truth: *Ownership is about attachment.* When we feel attached to a cause, to an organization, or even to another person, we will assume personal responsibility for the cause. People don't mind owning a problem that matters to them. They'll rack their heads, put in the hours, show up to meetings—all because they feel like they have a stake in the outcome. Skin in the game. Short of feeling invested, they bail for the exits.

It's not always possible, of course, to feel attached to the task. Most of the students I know don't feel particularly attached to the periodic table. Or grammar exercises. Or multiplication sprints. The same goes for a great deal of the workforce. They probably don't love to crunch numbers, fill out spreadsheets, or make sales calls. They labor through them—not out of intrinsic joy but practical necessity. You could say that none of them really "owns" their work at all. So does that mean that a vast majority of children and adults will never experience the thrills of autonomy simply because they lack deep attachment?

Not necessarily.

A powerful way to tap someone's intrinsic need for significance is to provide a measure of choice. Effective teachers do it all the time, engaging students in self-directed activities while narrowing the limits of how the work gets done. You find it with diabetes patients, who manage their blood-sugar levels more effectively when given a variety of lifestyle choices instead of a single prescription. And parents who let their kids decide how and when to handle after-school duties avoid the confrontation of wills that might otherwise occur. In each of the cases, autonomy is built through the medium of choice.

This practice succeeds in the workplace as well. Using a model known as "job crafting," employees at Google innovated around their job descriptions by customizing tasks and responsibilities to match their interests and values. Spread across five different company divisions, including sales, operations, accounting, marketing, and human resources, these job crafters devised a map of how they'd like to modify their tasks while still keeping to the realities of their positions. (It's not like the accountants could suddenly swap out balance sheets for balance beams.) After watching them work with the self-styled responsibilities for six weeks, managers rated them as being happier—and more productive.

If we want feedforward to become an instrument for independence, the two most powerful words at our disposal aren't *do this* but *you choose*. That's what energized the Momentous parents to plan their engagement nights and what motivated the factory-floor employees at Hawthorne Works back in chapter 1. Laying out the possibilities but letting others pick the actions sends a clear message that we trust their judgment. More important, it will let them experience the thrills of choice and voice, feeding their innate search for significance and leading to more satisfying—and self-sustaining—work outcomes.

FEEDBACK AND INCENTIVES: AUTONOMY KILLER #1

So if this is how you build autonomy—in the classroom, around the workplace, and even within your family—then why do we always seem to blow it?

It may have to do with our dependence on incentives. Employers love to dangle all kinds of performance sweeteners, from big-money bonuses and free vacations to profit sharing and use of company planes and cars. Incentives aren't all bad, of course. They get us to do the tasks that aren't inherently appealing, especially those that are routinized and noncomplex. And when those extrinsic motivators—be they carrots or sticks—become internalized values that are integrated into one's sense of self, research shows that they can actually yield a positive motivational effect. As a stand-alone practice, though, incentives are a punitive form of feedback that holds people back from becoming independent performers—and causes their work to suffer along the way.

To test whether very high monetary rewards actually decreased performance, economists from three schools of business management conducted a series of experiments at MIT, at the University of Chicago, and in rural India. They randomly assigned participants to work on a variety of tasks requiring motor coordination, concentration, or creativity and told the group they'd be paid based on how well they performed, keeping with their usual earnings. Not only that, but payments would also be bundled in different amounts—a day's pay, two weeks' pay, or five months' pay.

Based on what they stood to make, you might expect a good deal of variable performance. But for the most part, that didn't happen. Even with the incentives, the low- and middle-pay groups performed almost identically across all tasks, despite their degrees of difficulty. What's more, the high-pay group actually performed *worse* than the others. Even the prospect of significant rewards—nearly half a year's pay—couldn't unlock their capacity for complex, problem-based thinking. In fact, it drove it even further underground.

When feedback is tied to rewards, it fails. This is particularly true when it comes to kids. Most teachers realize that their job is to craft the "total child," which covers not just knowledge and skills but also actions and beliefs. Rewards may help short-term knowledge acquisition but hinder long-term attitudes toward learning. When we bribe students with gold stars, saturate them with prizes, and tempt them with point systems, we commoditize education and reduce effort to wish fulfillment. This creates an artificial prop for learning that makes students less prepared to conquer tasks on their own once the incentives dry up.

A good case in point is the Capital Gains project, a high-profile experiment in the use of educational incentives. Conceived by Harvard economist Roland Fryer, the four-city, $6.3 million study assessed whether financial incentives could spur academic achievement in urban classrooms. Second graders in Dallas received $2 for reading a book. Chicago high school freshmen were paid every five weeks for earning good grades in five core courses. Fourth and seventh graders in New York City earned cash payments for performing well on tests.

From 2007 to 2009, Capital Gains distributed a total of $9.4 million in cash incentives to twenty-seven thousand students. The program was built on a rather audacious assumption: Deep down, kids actually wanted to read books, earn good grades, and do well on tests. All that was missing was a motivator—something to help them overcome the gap that separates pure intentions from poor performance. And for the most part, people accepted its premise. Capital Gains was a media sensation. Fryer lined up support from foundations and corporations. Teachers were talking about it. And judging by their initial status reports, participating schools had found a promising way to reach the most underserved students in the system.

Or so they thought.

After eight months of trials, students who had received a financial reward showed no gain in their math scores. Worse, their reading scores actually *dropped*. "The impact of financial incentives on student achievement," Fryer reported, "is statistically zero in each city." In cases when performance did go up, it belonged to students with the highest levels of motivation, not those who lacked it. Ironically, the population most in need of the intervention never ended up receiving it.

As Daniel Pink showed in *Drive*, rewards only help when the task is simple and the motivation is low, and even then its effects are short-lived. Complex, people-centered problems aren't going to be solved by handing out gift cards or concert tickets. Incentives are often shiny but rarely substantive. Instead of hollowing out room for growth, they end up making us feel hollow inside, wanting and waiting for more. That's hardly a path to independence, which can only be experienced by seeing life on soberer terms: deep, difficult, and sometimes discouraging.

Autonomy is filled through the slow drip of effort. Traditional feedback, with its reliance on instant rewards, produces short-term success that goes as quickly as it comes. But feedforward plays the long game. It avoids the quick fixes and instant thrills and sets others up to do the hard work of working hard. Sharpening this message, especially for kids at a young age, is how we get them to resist the urge for quickness and shortcuts, especially when it comes to the important things in life: work, learning, friendship, love. Thinking back to two of the three Ss, there seems to be a strong correlation between them: We sweat over significant things.

FEEDBACK AND PRAISE: AUTONOMY KILLER #2

Are kids today more brittle than before?

If they do lack toughness, it's probably the result of what David Brooks calls "greater praise and greater honing." And parents have mostly themselves to blame for that. "Children are bathed in love, but it is often directional love," he claims, referring to the high cost, in both dollars and sanity, of raising children who are overly groomed by their parent handlers.

I know what Brooks means. In my line of work, I get to see quite a few parent-child interactions, and lately they smack of smothering. The feedback that parents share with their kids is meant either to coddle or to curate—to smooth out their children's feelings or to outfit them for their next step. Neither approach really prepares kids to handle challenges on their own or to think through decisions without someone else whispering in their ear. Worse, it's complicating the way young people perceive success—and, to a larger extent, themselves.

Every year, researchers at UCLA conduct a nationwide survey of college freshmen to gauge their values. In 1966, 42 percent said becoming rich was an important life goal. A generation later, in 1990, the number ballooned to 74 percent. You could slice that bump a few ways: Increased cost of living. A generational drift toward consumerism. Or something completely different— the growing infatuation with the self.

Maybe the newfound fascination with wealth had less to do with the economy and more to do with *expectations*—the students' feeling that they were somehow entitled to riches. Having been told practically since birth how wonderful, talented, and breathtakingly special they are, collegians in 1990 felt no hesitation in admitting something that, in an earlier age, would never go past the point of private thought. Going on the record about it, and with such striking candor, was something not seen before.

A decade later, a survey by Ernst & Young found that 65 percent of college and university students expected to become millionaires. Not wanted. *Expected.* Among them, 30 percent intended to achieve this goal by the time they turned forty. "Young people entering the workforce today seem very confident about their abilities to succeed in their careers," said James Freer, a former Ernst & Young executive, now retired from the firm.

That kind of unchecked confidence doesn't appear overnight. It's honed and pressed over time. And in today's culture of helicopter parenting, it seems to be baked into the feedback that kids routinely receive—layered with expectations, topped with praise. Thanks to pioneering and popular work by Stanford psychologist Carol Dweck, we now know that this kind of praise—the type that focuses on product, not process—leads people to adopt a fixed view of their performance and potential. Unfortunately, that's not something that goes away with time. As the fixed-growth mind-set hardens into adulthood, the same frailty that came to mark childhood will resurface in the workplace, with predictably similar results.

Unless, of course, we pull ourselves off the praise wheel and start to give feedback that is focused on supreme effort, not supreme talent. Because talent is native, there's not much value in rehashing it. Those natural gifts appear and stay automatically—which is why traditional feedback that praises talent tends to reinforce a fixed-performance mind-set. But feedforward lauds effort, not talent. And since effort is grown, not born, making that the focus of feedback teaches kids two things: First, and most promising, they can earn their own success. That's life changing. Second—and this is the bitter pill— they will fall down along the way. A lot. When it comes to effort, there is no guarantee of a victory lap, just a steady stride toward the goal. Each attempt brings us a little closer to it, but never uniformly.

For kids and adults alike, that means getting comfortable with the idea of failure—and recognizing that every pioneer, innovator, trailblazer, and disrupter stumbled on their way to success. That can be a difficult lesson to digest, even for older people, as the musicians from the strivers versus naturals study can attest.

From an early age, we angle for success—the right schools, the best grades, the strongest connections. We try to cover up our flaws and hide the scratch marks that come with trying. And that mind-set carries into adulthood. The researchers who studied the musicians found that many of them lied about their age, practiced with the shades drawn, and took other deceptive measures to appear more gifted and flawless in other people's eyes. They were among the most accomplished pianists of their time. But they didn't want to be seen failing.

As it turns out, failure doesn't have to be fatal. In fact, failure is just progress by other means. Feedforward that is process-driven and growth-oriented reveals all the "fails" that dot the long road to success. And once the flaws are bared, they can become a baseline for future improvement. As more people embrace imperfection as a natural and expected part of life, the stigma of failure slowly wears off—it's just something that we "do." Kids, especially, will find great relief in knowing that they don't need to turn in unblemished performances all the time. "Too many kids today are looking for reinforcement from us with our feedback," says Jessica Lahey, a former teacher and the bestselling author of *The Gift of Failure*. "We're being tested—can our judgment be trusted?"

To prove her point, Lahey shows me the checklist taped to her refrigerator door. It's meant for her thirteen-year-old son, Finn, whose coming-of-age adventures are chronicled in her magnificent book. On today's agenda:

- Shower
- Brush teeth
- Take backpack
- Take lunch
- Feed Abby (the dog)
- Feed Lucky (the cat)

The list is simple, specific, and self-directed. Oh, and in case you're wondering, it's Finn, not his mother, who compiles it. Each time he checks another item off his list, he gains the confidence that comes with competence. "I could nag him about his responsibilities," Lahey shrugs, "or I could just show him that I think he's responsible." That's the choice we face with every feedback encounter.

Feedback can be praise-laden. It can be process-driven. But it cannot be both. Highlighting talent over effort does not provide meaningful feedback. It merely confirms what the receiver already knows: *I'm excellent at this. Of course I did a good job!* What people really need is meaningful information about what to do when things don't come as naturally, easily, or stress-free. They need a troubleshooting guide for when times get tough.

A great example of process-driven feedforward is the SE2R feedback model developed by Mark Barnes. Instead of scribbling a grade and some token comments on a piece of student work, Barnes adopts a four-part method that accounts for what students do, not who they are:

- Summarize
- Explain
- Redirect
- Resubmit

First, teachers briefly *summarize* what students accomplished, then *explain* in greater detail what worked well. Next, teachers and students engage in a two-way conversation that allows students to *redirect* their efforts, guided by an active feedforward process. Finally, students *resubmit* a revised version of their work, based on a combination of input, discussion, and action steps.

What you find here, in stark contrast to the praise movement, is a very deliberate emphasis on trying, not talent. And while this approach is often bumpier, Camille Farrington thinks it is much more empowering than the alternative. "A grade is not necessarily that helpful in terms of early feedback because all it tells you is where you fail in terms of the expectation," she says. "It doesn't necessarily tell you what you need to do, or what part of your work needs to improve." As kids learn how to fill in those gaps, hopefully on their own, we might even say this: When failure produces autonomy, it feels more like success.

GETTING PEOPLE TO GROW

Throughout the chapter, we looked at how feedforward can play to people's strengths and future prospects and how the three Ss of autonomy—support, sweat, and significance—help uncover a drive for independence. This is feedforward at its best: concentrated on the receiver, focused on the future, and centered around potential. It's what gives people the confidence to move from victims to creators and to stretch their capacities for better work and stronger relationships. To help them succeed, there are fixes that managers, teachers, and parents can make right now to pave the way. Here are some of them:

1. Show them you care.
2. Grow people, not policies.
3. Know the needs.

1 Show Them You Care

Before we take a giant leap toward independence, we want to know that there's someone standing by our side. Supportive relationships give people the confidence and netting to dare greatly, as we saw with the Momentous home visits. This leads to something called *self-efficacy*, or the belief that we are capable of performing a task on our own. And according to Albert Bandura, the researcher most associated with the theory, this belief grows stronger when we receive feedback from people we trust and respect. Their encouragement gives us the backing to persevere in the face of challenges.

Those gestures can come in all shapes and sizes—even as small as a Post-it note. In one study, teachers returned marked-up papers with two sets of comments. Some had generic statements like "good job" or "nice work," while others came with a Post-it note that read, "I'm giving you these comments because I have very high expectations and I know you can reach them." Researchers found that this small gesture paid big returns, especially for students of color: 72 percent voluntarily revised their papers, compared to just 17 percent of those who received the generic feedback message. In addition, the Post-it note group received better grades. Their willingness to grind out revisions shows a simple truth: We try when others care.

Giving feedback that communicates caring is part art, part smarts. Begin with some commonsense courtesies: Put away your phone. Make eye contact. Choose a comfortable setting, and, if possible, sit beside the other person, not across the table. Most of all, be timely. You'd be surprised by the number of people who told me that their number one association with feedback is waiting—as in waiting to actually receive follow-up feedback for a work project or lesson observation.

And then there's the art. Like we saw in chapter 2, sharing negative feedback may actually bring positive results, especially for more experienced employees. But it still needs to be delivered with a soft touch. Stick with feedforward that's Particular and Authentic—don't throw too much at another person at once, and make sure whatever hits the dashboard comes from a genuine place of understanding and honesty. Taking the time to size up what others really need is the surest way to show them you care.

2 Grow People, Not Policies

As we said before, letting go isn't marked by what we give up but by what we give. When we give others latitude over their lives, we put the reins back in their hands, which is exactly what happened when Momentous turned over engagement nights to the parents and when Google let its employees become job crafters. Like Genius Hour and the other creative breakthroughs we saw back in chapter 3, autonomy emerges from conditions that are flexed, not forced.

And it makes people happier, too, even when they have to work harder as a result. That's what two Wharton professors found after surveying more than thirty thousand alumni dating back to 1990. It turned out that the graduates who started their own companies were happier than their salaried peers, even after controlling for variables like earnings and years of experience. Despite the headaches and hassles that came with running their own businesses, entrepreneurs felt energized by the possibility of creating and filling their own professional space.

We can find ways to give others that same power and authority even in more highly structured school and work environments, but it takes a deliberate change in posture. At their core, organizations grow either policies or people—the things they will do *to* them or *for* them. It's easy to spot the difference. Take a typical meeting: When the agenda is filled up with documentation, governance issues, and other adminstrivia, that's an organization that puts its policies before its people. But when meetings wind up focusing on field discussions, learning opportunities, and collaborative conversations, you know the organization puts its people and their potential first. Talking about autonomy is one thing, but helping people step into it is another.

3 Know the Needs

Sometimes, we line our feedback with pointed expectations for improvement. "Now that we've talked about this," a supervisor might begin, "I'd really like to see you put this to work next time around." But simply putting out a target, without actually providing the right tools to strike it, rarely leads to hits. Feedforward does more than just describe a flaw and prescribe the fix. It focuses on what people actually need—like whether they could stand to benefit from additional training, on-the-job support, or just more time to work. Asking someone "Do you have what you need to be successful here?" isn't just a token gesture. It could quite literally expose the reality gap that separates what we think others have and what they actually possess.

That information imbalance is sometimes called the "curse of knowledge." It happens when we wrongly assume, based on what we know, that others must know it, too. We forget what it's like *not* to have that knowledge, which causes us to be more abstract and less forgiving in our delivery of information. As the "experts," we take mastery for granted and skate over context and details. When we talk, the information we release is only a fraction of what we actually hold. The problem isn't that we treat ourselves as superiors. It's that we treat others as equals.

Say, for instance, you're asked to choose a popular song like "Happy Birthday" and tap out the rhythm of the melody with your fingers. To the tapper, the beat is so familiar and universal that anyone listening should be able to guess it. But when researchers actually put this to the test, almost no one listening along could name that tune. Out of 120 popular songs performed by tappers, only three—a measly 2.5 percent—were correctly identified by listeners. But the more surprising discovery: Tappers assumed that listeners would label half of the songs correctly, an overestimate of twenty-fold. Talk about a curse of knowledge! To the tappers, who had the melody playing in their heads, the taps had meaning. But for the listeners, who lacked the same context, the taps were just indiscriminate noise.

To sidestep that problem, feedforward has to double down on specifics. Dan and Chip Heath, authors of *Made to Stick*, suggest that feedback givers speak in concrete language. Directing someone to "maximize shareholder value" isn't concrete, but urging them to "increase weekly sales by 3 percent" is. Traditional feedback that is vague and imprecise is hard to understand and leads to second-guessing and uneasiness—*What is this person trying to tell me, anyway?* But feedforward that is plain-spoken, targeted, and specific issues a clear call to action that anyone can grasp. It puts a goal in within reach and helps people start moving toward it. When there's clarity about what was said and needs to be done, people aren't afraid to start moving on their own.

■   ■   ■

"People have a pretty good tape of their shortcomings running in the background," says Michelle Kinder, rolling a glitter ball between her fingers. "The last thing they need is someone else adding layers to it." With feedforward, we help other people write their own song but stand back and let them play it for themselves. They might miss a note here and there. It might take a while to learn the melody. But as long as we calibrate our feedback to set the right expectations, provide the right amount of support, and demonstrate the right intent, we'll give others the courage and confidence to compose the best soundtracks of their lives.

Conclusion

Building Something More Useful

About two weeks before my book deadline, I had a performance review. In the private education sector, where I've spent my entire career, these are mostly casual encounters—more like a conversation, really. The review process is typically based on anecdotal evidence: classroom observations, feedback from parents, chatter among colleagues. The picture is a lot more complex in public schools, where high-stakes testing and value-added evaluations tie student achievement to teacher performance, often putting jobs on the line.

Over the years, I've come to see the review as a benevolent necessity, like taking your car for its annual inspection. There's a routine check to make sure everything's in good working order, followed by some obligatory paperwork, then off you go. Had there been a true cause for concern—some kink in the system or a malfunctioning part—chances are it would have shown up by now. Teacher reviews, like car inspections, don't tell us something new; they merely confirm what we know, which is why—short of a performance bombshell—lots of people just shuffle through it. Reviews come and go, most of the time quickly and painlessly, something to finish and then forget about—until next year rolls around, when you do it all over again.

But this time felt different. As it happened, I was putting the finishing touches on this book and getting ready to send it off for final edits, having just spent the better part of a year immersed in the topic of giving and receiving feedback. I had read everything on the subject. I had met top executives who were reinventing performance management and changing the face of feedback. And now, sitting on the other side of a performance review, holding a piece of paper that reduced my efforts to a series of line items and checkboxes, I felt, well, a little shortchanged.

The page was a neatly ordered re-creation of my past. There were sections for "strengths" and "management style." A shaded area contained indicators for improvement. My supervisor's comments, written in half-cursive shorthand, appeared just below that, right beside the line where she affixed her signature and I was expected to place my own. Nowhere in the form did it talk about "future actions" or "next steps." It stopped short of assigning a rating, but it communicated something just as final—what I had done and could not undo. It was, in all respects, a permanent referendum on my past.

We chatted briefly about the contents of the review, which were mostly positive, and wrapped up with polite conversation. I thanked her for her time and left. As the day went on, I forgot about the form, which disappeared between a stack of reading materials and some graded papers in my work bag. But at home that night, during a quiet moment, I did something I can't ever recall doing before.

I read it again.

This time, I tried to forensically reconstruct all the formative moments from the past year: interactions with students, conversations with parents, the times when lessons went according to plan and the times they utterly fell apart. Some of it registered. Most did not. A thick assortment of highs and lows, triumphs and failures, breakthroughs and breakdowns, seized moments and missed opportunities—all of it just settled into a hazy, semicoherent picture of what I did over many months. Or, to be more exact, what I *thought* I did.

Truthfully, I couldn't remember it all. At least not the way it probably happened at the time. Few people could.

We like to say that hindsight is 20/20, but I think it's more like 50/50—as in a 50/50 chance that we'll actually be able to look back on past events and remember, relive, reorder, and retell episodes with fidelity to the facts. From the moment we first gather new information—articles we read, conversations we have, events we experience—we start to forget it. So when it came time to retrieve the highlights and lowlights of a year gone by, the best I could do was imagine things the way they were or should have been.

To hold on to information, we need to "interrupt the process of forgetting," which is how Peter Brown, Henry Roediger, and Mark McDaniel elegantly put it in their book, *Make It Stick: The Science of Successful Learning*. The trick, they argue, is to allow memory retrieval to kick in shortly after new information has settled but just before it begins to recede. Because if we wait too long to revisit what we've learned, it will have left us for good.

Looking back at that form, I realized the problem with my review wasn't the tone. It was the timing. The feedback it contained had arrived too late. Instead of landing in intervals, it came crashing down all at once, which meant that I was now stuck in reverse, overwhelmed by information that literally had no potential or future prospects.

Feedback that suffers from time lapse keeps us from moving forward. And if it's happening to me, chances are it's happening to you, too.

■   ■   ■

Throughout this book, we followed dramatic story lines: turnarounds and comebacks, change agents and revolutionaries. Some of these grew out of individual heroics; others emerged as courageous ensembles. The action crisscrossed continents and spread from board rooms to classrooms and even to dining rooms, but it never strayed far from a simple and stubborn truth: People can't change what they can't control. If we want them to make meaningful improvements in their lives, then the feedback we share has to point to a future they can control, not a past they can't.

Looking to the past.

Looking to the future.

Where do you want the people in your professional and personal circles to be looking?

If you want to help another person become more creative, develop more consciousness, discover purpose in work and work with purpose—if you want the people who report to you, learn from you, and look up to you to deliver the very best of their performance and potential and start filling their space the way they best know how—then you have to feedforward. The alternative is constricted, unfocused, aimless, and adrift. It belongs to a time that is forever lost. And when we push people back to the past, they get lost, too.

Making the move from past to prologue isn't easy. It requires a reordering of our priorities—a deliberate shift from ratings to people and evaluation to development—and a new toolkit for talking to people in a way that increases their capacity for self-knowledge, mastery, and purpose. Because these tools provide a much-needed fix to traditional feedback, they are part of a REPAIR plan—the six dimensions of feedforward that change the way we conduct everyday conversations with the people closest to us.

Whether the interactions are taking place between managers and their reports, teachers and their students, or individuals and their loved ones, the strategies we outlined in these pages can apply in virtually any setting. And they work, too, based on stories recounted here and elsewhere of people who use them to strengthen their communication, improve their relationships, and cut across the noise to find what they are looking for.

But to reach full impact, feedforward has to be more than just a method. It must become a mind-set: a decision to break free from the bonds of traditional feedback, reject its demanding and demoralizing tone, and diminish the size and strength of our own voices to make it possible for others to discover their own.

When we start sharing feedforward, we might be surprised to learn that the one thing keeping us from getting what we always wanted is giving others what they truly needed: timely, future-looking messages that speak to their prospects, not their past. In its traditional form, feedback is a weapon of fear. But reimagined as feedforward, it can quickly become an instrument of joy—full of potential, brimming with hope, resonating with possibility. All we need to do is learn a different set of chords and let others follow the rhythm. Because when that change plays out, it's a beautiful thing to hear.

Notes

INTRODUCTION

3   **flapped right off the page**   The swallowtail diagrams—all drawn by Austin himself—are shared with permission by EL Education and the Anser Charter School in Boise, Idaho. To watch a video about Austin's butterfly, visit http://modelsofexcellence.eleducation.org/resources/austins-butterfly.

4   **people apply just 30 percent of the feedback they receive**   Scott Halford, "Five Steps for Giving Productive Feedback," *Entrepreneur*, November 10, 2014, retrieved August 5, 2016, www.entrepreneur.com/article/219437.

5   **customer-experience surveys**   Research about customer aversions to giving feedback at hotels and supermarkets can be found in Chezy Ofir and Itamar Simonson, "In Search of Negative Customer Feedback: The Effect of Expecting to Evaluate on Satisfaction Evaluations," *Journal of Marketing Research* 38 (2001): 170–82, and Chezy Ofir and Itamar Simonson, "The Effect of Stating Expectations on Customer Satisfaction and Shopping Experience," *Journal of Marketing Research* 44 (2007): 164–74.

5   **demonstrate less interest in learning**   These include Carl Benware and Edward Deci, "Quality of Learning with an Active Versus Passive Motivational Set," *American Educational Research Journal* 21 (1984): 755–65; Wendy Grolnick and Richard Ryan, "Autonomy in Children's Learning: An Experimental and Individual Difference Investigation," *Journal of Personality and Social Psychology* 52 (1987): 890–98; and Masaharu Kage, "The Effects of Evaluation on Intrinsic Motivation" (paper presented at the meeting of the Japan Association of Educational Psychology, Joetsu, Japan, 1991).

6   **you can't kick an old habit**   Roy Baumeister, Kathleen Vohs, and Diane Tice,
      "The Strength Model of Self-Control," *Current Directions in Psychological
      Science* 16 (2007): 351–55.

6   **"successful people love getting ideas for the future"**   Marshall Goldsmith,
      What Got You Here Won't Get You There (New York: Hyperion, 2007), 174.

CHAPTER 1

14   **"All of the things"**   Ashley Goodall, personal interview, May 6, 2016. All of
      this chapter's subsequent quotations from Goodall come from this interview
      unless otherwise noted. Deloitte's reinvention of performance management
      is chronicled by Marcus Buckingham and Ashley Goodall, "Reinventing
      Performance Management," *Harvard Business Review*, April 2015.

16   **more about the person giving the rating**   The discussion of idiosyncratic
      rater effect and the subsequent study that confirmed it can be found in Steven
      Scullen and Michael Mount, "Understanding the Latent Structure of Job
      Performance Ratings," *Journal of Applied Psychology* 85 (2010): 956–70.

17   **neurotransmitters in our brains**   For more on this topic, see David Rock,
      *Your Brain at Work: Strategies for Overcoming Distraction, Regaining Focus,
      and Working Smarter All Day Long* (New York: HarperBusiness, 2009).

17   **"learned helplessness"**   Groundbreaking field research can be found in
      Martin Seligman, "Learned Helplessness," *Annual Review of Medicine* 23
      (1972): 407–12.

18   **85 percent of HR managers**   See, for example, Jenna McGregor, "The
      Corporate Kabuki of Performance Reviews," *Washington Post*, February 14, 2013,
      retrieved August 11, 2015, www.washingtonpost.com/national/on-leadership/
      the-corporate-kabuki-of-performance-reviews/2013/02/14/59b60e86-7624-
      11e2-aa12-e6cf1d31106b_story.html.

20   **"rank and yank"**   For a brief history of "rank and yank" practices, see Leslie
      Kwoh, "Rank and Yank Retains Vocal Fans," *Wall Street Journal*, January 31,
      2012, retrieved August 6, 2015, www.wsj.com/articles/SB100014240529702033
      6350457718697006437522.

CHAPTER 2

25   **"Not the Four Seasons"**   Mike Preston, personal interview, July 7, 2016. All
      of this chapter's subsequent quotations from Preston come from this interview
      unless otherwise noted.

27   **According to one recent survey**   Deloitte, "Business Needs to Reset Its
      Purpose to Attract Millennials, according to Deloitte's Annual Survey," press

release, January 14, 2015, www2.deloitte.com/global/en/pages/about-deloitte/
articles/2015-millennial-survey-press-release.html.

28   **"psychological ownership"** James B. Avey, Bruce Avolio, Craig Crossley,
      and Fred Luthans, "Psychological Ownership: Theoretical Extensions,
      Measurement, and Relation to Work Outcomes," *Journal of Organizational
      Behavior* 30 (2009): 173–91.

28   **employees under the age of twenty-five** Quantum Workplace, *2014
      Employee Recognition Trends Report*, available at www.quantumworkplace.
      com/resources/whitepapers/research-and-trends/2014-recognition-trends
      -report/.

28   **nine in ten executives rate engagement** More information about the survey
      can be found at http://dupress.com/periodical/trends/human-capital-trends/.
      The earlier 2015 report can be viewed at https://dupress.deloitte.com/dup-us
      -en/focus/human-capital-trends/2015.html.

29   **research conducted by Gallup** Steve Crabtree, "Worldwide, 13% of Employees
      Are Engaged at Work," Gallup, October 8, 2013, retrieved July 15, 2016, www
      .gallup.com/poll/165269/worldwide-employees-engaged-work.aspx.

30   **definitely not child's play** Claire Malone, "The Serious Business of Animated
      Films, by the Numbers," *New York Times Style Magazine*, October 20, 2015.

30   **twenty facial expressions** Shichuan Du, Yong Tao, and Aleix Martinez,
      "Compound Facial Expressions of Emotion," *Proceedings of the National
      Academy of Sciences* 111 (2014): 1454–62.

32   **"A competitive approach"** Ed Catmull, *Creativity, Inc.: Overcoming the
      Unseen Forces That Stand in the Way of True Inspiration* (New York: Random
      House, 2012), 101–2.

33   **second-worst place to drive** As reported in the 2016 TomTom traffic index,
      available at www.tomtom.com. In case you're wondering, Mexico City has the
      worst traffic of any major city in the world.

33   **even after the group was disbanded** Charlan Nemeth, Bernard Personnaz,
      Marie Personnaz, and Jack Goncalo, "The Liberating Role of Conflict in Group
      Creativity: A Study in Two Countries," *European Journal of Social Psychology*
      34 (2004): 365–74.

34   **there's one stat** Mark Medina, "Lakers' Kobe Bryant Serves as Mentor for
      Several of NBA's Young Stars, Role Players," *LA Daily News*, December 13,
      2014, retrieved July 14, 2016, www.dailynews.com/sports/20141213/lakers-kobe
      -bryant-serves-as-mentor-for-several-nbas-young-stars-role-players.

35   **"I think he enjoys seeing"** Bob Garcia, "Lakers' Kobe Bryant Is Finally
      Relishing His Mentor Role," *About Sports*, December 16, 2015, retrieved July

14, 2016, http://lalakers.about.com/od/Player-Bios/fl/Lakers-Kobe-Bryant-is-finally-relishing-mentor-role.htm.

35   **more selective approach**   Mark Medina, "Kobe Bryant's Teammates Appreciate His Feedback on the Bench," *LA Daily News*, March 11, 2015, retrieved July 14, 2016, www.insidesocal.com/lakers/2015/03/11/kobe-bryants-teammates-appreciate-his-feedback-on-the-bench/.

36   **"people start making stupid mistakes"**   Sharon Begley, "The Science of Making Decisions," *Newsweek*, February 27, 2011, retrieved August 30, 2016, www.newsweek.com/science-making-decisions-68627.

36   **"decision fatigue"**   Shai Danziger, Jonathan Levav, and Liora Avnaim-Pesso, "Extraneous Factors in Judicial Decisions," *Proceedings of the National Academy of Sciences* 108 (2011): 6889–92.

37   **decision shortcuts**   Ned Augenblick and Scott Nicholson, "Ballot Position, Choice Fatigue, and Voter Behaviour," *Review of Economic Studies* 83 (2016): 460–80.

39   **three-to-one margin**   Jack Zenger and Joseph Folkman, "Your Employees Want the Negative Feedback You Hate to Give," *Harvard Business Review*, January 15, 2014, retrieved July 2, 2016, https://hbr.org/2014/01/your-employees-want-the-negative-feedback-you-hate-to-give?referral=00060.

39   **experts on a subject**   Stacey Finkelstein and Ayelet Fishbach, "Tell Me What I Did Wrong: Experts Seek and Respond to Negative Feedback," *Journal of Consumer Research* 39 (2012): 22–38.

40   **people tend to remember**   Dirk Steiner and Jeffrey Rain, "Immediate and Delayed Primacy and Recency Effects in Performance Evaluation," *Journal of Applied Psychology* 74 (1989): 136–42.

40   **"feedback wrap"**   Jurgen Appelo, "Ditch the Praise Sandwich, Make Feedback Wraps," *Forbes*, August 17, 2015, retrieved July 27, 2016, www.forbes.com/sites/jurgenappelo/2015/08/17/ditch-the-praise-sandwich-make-feedback-wraps/#40b0c8064ef3.

42   **negative patient feedback**   The Cleveland Clinic's struggles with patient experience—and its ultimate turnaround—is chronicled by James Merlino and Ananth Ramen, "Health Care's Service Fanatics," *Harvard Business Review*, May 2013.

44   **"shrinking the change"**   Dan and Chip Heath, *Switch: How to Change Things When Change Is Hard* (New York: Broadway Books, 2010).

45   **teacher effectiveness on student learning**   See, for example, William Sanders and June Rivers, *Cumulative and Residual Effects of Teachers on Future Student Academic Achievement, Research Progress Report* (Knoxville: University of

Tennessee, 1996). The multiyear study showed that when children, beginning in third grade, were placed with three high-performing teachers in a row, they scored, on average, in the ninety-sixth percentile on Tennessee's statewide mathematics assessment at the end of fifth grade. When children with comparable achievement histories were placed with three low-performing teachers in a row starting in third grade, their average score on the same mathematics assessment was in the forty-fourth percentile, an enormous fifty-two percentile point difference for children who presumably had comparable abilities and skills.

45   **Teachers who are actively coached**   Bruce Joyce and Beverly Showers, "Staff Development and Student Learning: A Synthesis of Research on Models of Teaching," *Educational Leadership* 45 (1987): 11–23.

47   **the Nest Learning Thermostat arrived**   The story behind Nest's launch is recounted by Tom Simonite, "How Nest's Control Freaks Reinvented the Thermostat," *MIT Technology Review*, February 15, 2013. The company's unique approach to building the device is chronicled by Rich Kaarlgaard and Michael Malone, *Team Genius: The New Science of High-Performing Organizations* (New York: HarperBusiness, 2016).

47   **"creative abrasion"**   Dorothy Leonard and Susann Straus, "Putting Your Company's Whole Brain to Work," *Harvard Business Review* 75 (1997): 110–22.

50   **no team can flourish**   Marcus Buckingham, "What Great Managers Do," *Harvard Business Review*, March 2005, http://hbr.org/2005/03/what-great-managers-do/ar/.

50   **they guessed it to be less steep**   Simone Schnall, Kent D. Harber, Jeanine K. Stefanucci, and Dennis R. Proffitt, "Social Support and the Perception of Geographical Slant," *Journal of Experimental Social Psychology* 44 (2008): 1246–55.

CHAPTER 3

57   **"I saw it as an opportunity"**   Elad Segev, personal interview, July 21, 2015. All of this chapter's subsequent quotations from Segev come from this interview unless otherwise noted.

61   **They simply ate the wafers**   Details of this experiment are captured in Elad Segev's TEDxHIT talk, "The Chemistry of Creativity," which can be found at www.youtube.com/watch?v=Jk0AknXMXmc.

64   **"That's why so many insights"**   The creative power of alpha waves in the brain's right hemisphere is explored by Jonah Lehrer, *Imagine: How Creativity Works* (Boston: Houghton-Mifflin Harcourt, 2012). The quote from Bhattacharya appears on page 31.

66   **make students different, not the same**   Groundbreaking work in the field of multiple intelligences has been carried out by Harvard University psychologist Howard Gardner and operationalized by Carol Ann Tomlinson of the University of Virginia under the framework of "differentiated instruction."

68   **"They're not going to have teachers"**   Personal interview, February 13, 2016.

69   **"Students love the freedom"**   Personal interview, February 15, 2016.

70   **double standard among management**   Todd Kashdan, "Companies Value Curiosity But Stifle It Anyway," *Harvard Business Review*, October 21, 2015, retrieved October 25, 2015, https://hbr.org/2015/10/companies-value-curiosity -but-stifle-it-anyway.

71   **there's no shortcut to eureka**   K. Anders Ericson, Ralf Th. Krampe, and Clemens Tesch-Römer, "The Role of Deliberate Practice in the Acquisition of Expert Performance," *Psychological Review* 100 (1993): 363–406.

72   **disappointment had become a catalyst**   Modupe Akinola and Wendy Beres Mendes, "The Dark Side of Creativity: Biological Vulnerability and Negative Emotions Lead to Greater Artistic Creativity," *Personality and Social Psychology Bulletin* 34 (2008): 1677–86.

CHAPTER 4

76   **"The people I work with"**   Michael Gervais, personal interview, December 10, 2015. All of this chapter's subsequent quotations from Gervais come from this interview unless otherwise noted.

77   **"It's the most fascinating culture"**   The quote comes from Matthew Futterman, "The Shrink on the Seattle Seahawks' Sideline," *Wall Street Journal*, January 27, 2015, www.wsj.com/articles/the-shrink-on-the-seattle-seahawks-sideline-1422402204.

82   **189 senior managers**   Steven Rogelberg, Logan Justice, Phillip Braddy, et al., "The Executive Mind: Leader Self-Talk, Effectiveness and Strain," *Journal of Managerial Psychology* 28 (2013): 183–201.

84   **Physical therapists have used motor imagery**   Ruth Dickstein and Judith E. Deutsch, "Motor Imagery in Physical Therapist Practice," *Physical Therapy* 87 (2007): 942–53.

84   **learning how to throw darts**   Antonis Hatzigeorgiadis, Nikos Zourbanos, Evangelos Galanis, and Yiannis Theodorakis, "Self-Talk and Sports Performance: A Meta-analysis," *Perspectives on Psychological Science* 6 (2011): 348–56.

84   **study of elite sprinters**   Clifford Mallet and Stephanie Hanrahan, "Applied Research Race Modeling: An Effective Cognitive Strategy for the 100m Sprinter?" *Sports Psychologist* 11 (2012): 72–85.

85   **coined a non-enlightenment version**   Jon Kabat-Zinn, *Wherever You Go, There You Are: Mindfulness Meditation in Everyday Life* (New York: Hyperion, 1994).

85   **associations between mindfulness and physical health**   Kayloni Olsen and Charles Emery, "Mindfulness and Weight Loss: A Systematic Review," *Psychosomatic Medicine* 77 (2015): 59–67.

85   **costliest natural disaster in U.S. history**   At $108 billion in domestic damage, Hurricane Katrina was by far the United States' costliest natural disaster based on tracking done by the National Hurricane Center. See Eric S. Blake, Christopher W. Landsea, and Ethan J. Gibney, "The Deadliest, Costliest, and Most Intense United States Tropical Cyclones from 1851 to 2010 (and Other Frequently Requested Hurricane Facts)," National Hurricane Center, National Oceanic and Atmospheric Administration, accessed January 23, 2016, www. nhc.noaa.gov/pdf/nws-nhc-6.pdf.

85   **workers showed significant reduction**   Daphne Davis and Jeffrey Hayes, "What Are the Benefits of Mindfulness? A Practice Review of Psychotherapy-Related Research," *Psychotherapy* 48 (2011): 198–208.

86   **unleash more creativity around the workplace**   For more on mindfulness in the workplace, see Kimberly Schaufenbuel, "Why Google, Target, and General Mills Are Investing in Mindfulness," *Harvard Business Review*, December 28, 2015, retrieved December 29, 2015, https://hbr.org/2015/12/why-google-target -and-general-mills-are-investing-in-mindfulness. The topic is also covered by Mike Hughlett, "Mindfulness Arrives at the Workplace," *Minneapolis Star Tribune*, November 24, 2013, retrieved January 19, 2016, www.startribune.com/ mindfulness-arrives-in-the-twin-cities-workplace/233176121.

87   **Stress in America survey**   The results are taken from the 2009 *Stress in America* report by the American Psychological Association, retrieved January 20, 2016, www.apa.org/news/press/releases/stress/2009/stress-exec-summary .pdf.

88   **soft skills can translate into hard gains**   Kimberly Schonert-Reichl, Eva Oberle, Molly Stewart Lawlor, David Abbott, Kimberly Thomson, Tim Oberlander, and Adele Diamond, "Enhancing Cognitive and Social-Emotional Development through a Simple-to-Administer Mindfulness-Based School Program for Elementary School Children: A Randomized Controlled Trial," *Developmental Psychology* 51 (2015): 52–66. To measure the MindUP program's effectiveness on stress physiology, researchers from the University of British Columbia collected saliva from the children to analyze their cortisol levels, a stress indicator. They relied on peer and self-reporting and also measured the children's cognitive abilities, including their memory, concentration, and focus.

90   **people with spider phobias**   Katharina Kircanski, Matthew Lieberman, and Michelle Craske, "Feelings into Words: Contributions of Language to Exposure Therapy," *Psychological Science* 23 (2012): 1086–91.

90   **high multitaskers . . . took longer to switch tasks**   Faria Sana, Tina Weston, and Nicholas Cepeda, "Laptop Multitasking Hinders Classroom Learning for Both Users and Nearby Peers," *Computers & Education* 62 (2013): 24–31. Researchers found that participants who multitasked on a laptop during a lecture scored lower on a test compared to those who did not multitask. So did participants who sat within direct view of a multitasking peer.

91   **more of a time-killer**   Eyal Ophir, Clifford Nass, and Anthony Wagner, "Cognitive Control in Media-Multitaskers," *Proceedings of the National Academies of Sciences in the United States* 106 (2009): 15583–87.

91   **changed their mood meters**   Richard Davidson, Jon Kabat-Zinn, Jessica Schumacher, Melissa Rosenkranz, Daniel Muller, Saki Santorelli, Ferris Urbanowski, Anne Harringon, Katherine Bonus, and John Sheridan, "Alterations in Brain and Immune Function Produced by Mindfulness Meditation," *Psychosomatic Medicine* 65 (2003): 564–70.

92   **we've formed a new habit**   Charles Duhigg, *The Power of Habit: Why We Do What We Do in Life and Business* (New York: Random House, 2013).

92   **"Our deepest fear"**   Marianne Williamson, *A Return to Love* (New York: HarperCollins, 1992), 190.

CHAPTER 5

96   **"We're not in the business of short-term"**   Rand Stagen, personal interview, October 28, 2015, and December 28, 2015. All of this chapter's subsequent quotations from Stagen come from this interview unless otherwise noted.

98   **more connected mobile devices than actual human beings**   PR Newswire, "Number of Active Mobile Devices Surpasses World Population," *The Business Journals*, October 6, 2014, retrieved March 6, 2016, www.bizjournals.com/prnewswire/press_releases/2014/10/06/NY30877.

99   **becoming good servants**   A fuller treatment of the servant's attitude can be found in the landmark work by Robert Greenleaf, *Servant Leadership: A Journey into the Nature of Legitimate Power and Greatness*, 25th ed. (New York: Paulist Press, 2002).

100   **"Well-run, values-centered businesses"**   Raj Sisodia and his colleagues identified twenty-eight companies (eighteen of which are publicly held) on the basis of these qualities. They found that conscious companies outperformed the S&P 500 Index by fourteen times and good to great companies by six times

based on cumulative returns over a period of fifteen years (1998–2013). More information about the performance power of Conscious Capitalism is explored in John Mackey and Raj Sisodia, *Conscious Capitalism: Liberating the Heroic Spirit of Business* (Boston: Harvard Business Review Press, 2013). The quote from Bill George appears page 4.

102 **an inescapable part of who we are**   Christopher Frith and Daniel Wolpert, eds., *The Neuroscience of Social Interactions: Decoding, Influencing and Imitating the Actions of Others* (Oxford: Oxford University Press, 2004).

103 **read and process social cues**   Greg Norman, Louise Hawkley, Steven Cole, and John Cacioppo, "Social Neuroscience: The Social Brain, Oxytocin, and Health," *Social Neuroscience* 7 (2012): 18–29.

103 **appetite for sociability**   Markus Heinrichs, Thomas Baumgartner, Clemes Kirschbaum, and Ulrike Ehlert, "Social Support and Oxytocin Interact to Suppress Cortisol and Subjective Responses to Psychosocial Stress," *Biological Psychiatry* 54 (2003): 1389–98.

104 **so-called mirror neurons**   Giacomo Rizzolati, "The Mirror Neuron System and Its Function in Humans," *Anatomical Embryology* 210 (2005): 419–21.

105 **"Deep in our architecture"**   The quote from Krulwich comes from an episode of PBS's *Nova*, "Mirror Neurons," originally aired on January 25, 2005.

106 **negative social cueing**   Marie Dasborough, "Cognitive Asymmetry in Employee Emotional Reactions to Leadership Behaviors," *Leadership Quarterly* 17 (2006): 163–78.

106 **state of mental paralysis**   David Rock, *Your Brain at Work: Strategies for Overcoming Distraction, Regaining Focus, and Working Smarter All Day Long* (New York: HarperBusiness, 2009).

108 **twice as likely to elicit laughter**   Daniel Goleman and Richard Boyatzis, "Social Intelligence and the Biology of Leadership," *Harvard Business Review* 86 (2008): 74–81.

108 **get more out of the people**   Sigal Barsade and Donald Gibson, "Why Does Affect Matter in Organisations?" *Academy of Management Perspectives* 21 (2007): 36–59. Leaders who appeared sad triggered feelings of doubt and increased analytical behaviors among employees, shifting the culture from one of self-growth to self-preservation.

109 **people felt iced out**   Kipling Williams, "Ostracism: The Impact of Being Rendered Meaningless," in *Meaning, Mortality, and Choice: The Social Psychology of Existential Concerns*, ed. Philip Shaver (Washington, DC: American Psychological Association, 2012), 309–23.

111   **two pizzas for lunch**   Information about the Ringlemann effect comes from https://en.wikipedia.org/wiki/Ringelmann_effect. For more on relational loss, see Jennifer Mueller, "Why Individuals in Larger Teams Perform Worse," *Organizational Behavior and Human Decision Processes* 117 (2012): 111–24. The negative inverse relationship between team size and individual performance occurred even when researchers controlled for extrinsic motivation and perceived coordination losses. Jeff Bezos's "two pizza" rule can be found at www.businessinsider.com/jeff-bezos-two-pizza-rule-for-productive-meetings-2013-10.

111   **became its secret weapon**   Patrick Laughlin, Erin Hatch, Jonathan Silver, and Lee Boh, "Groups Perform Better Than the Best Individuals on Letters-to-Numbers Problems: Effects of Group Size," *Journal of Personality and Social Psychology* 90 (2006): 644–51.

112   **better delayed post-test results**   Christine Howe, "Collaborative Group Work in Middle Childhood: Joint Instruction, Unresolved Contradiction and Growth of Knowledge," *Human Development* 52 (2009): 215–19.

113   **"psychological safety"**   Amy Edmonson, "Psychological Safety and Work Behavior in Teams," *Administrative Science Quarterly* 44 (1999): 350–83.

CHAPTER 6

117   **"hard for me to stay focused"**   Yolanda Mendoza, personal interview, June 17, 2016. All of this chapter's subsequent quotations from Mendoza come from this interview unless otherwise noted.

119   **road to better outcomes**   Information about the work of the Momentous Institute can be accessed at https://issuu.com/momentousinstitute/docs/mi_annual_report_2015.

121   **They're crushing them**   The growing disparity between college admission rates for low-income and high-income students is available through the National Student Clearinghouse Research Center, http://nscresearchcenter.org/hsbenchmarks2014/#Table7.

122   **"In the time of Google"**   Michelle Kinder, personal interview, June 17, 2016. All of this chapter's subsequent quotations from Kinder come from this interview unless otherwise noted.

123   **In an animal study**   Nicole Branan, "Stress Kills Brain Cells Off," *Scientific American*, June 1, 2007.

124   **"settle your glitter"**   Susan Kaiser Greenland, *The Mindful Child: How to Help Your Child Manage Stress and Become Happier, Kinder and More Compassionate* (New York: Free Press, 2011).

126 **"serve and return"** More information about "serve and return" interactions can be found at Harvard University's Center for the Developing Child, retrieved on March 31, 2016, https://developingchild.harvard.edu/science/key-concepts/serve-and-return.

127 **home-visiting interventions** Mary Dozier, Elizabeth Peloso, Oliver Lindhiem, et al., "Developing Evidence-Based Interventions for Foster Children: An Example of a Randomized Clinical Trial with Infants and Toddlers," *Journal of Social Issues* 62 (2006): 767–85.

129 **"academic perseverance"** Farrington's work on academic perseverance is profiled in Paul Tough, *Helping Children Succeed* (New York: Houghton-Mifflin Harcourt, 2016). For more on her work, see Camille Farrington, Melissa Roderick, Elaine Allensworth, Jenny Nagaoka, Tasha Seneca Keyes, David Johnson, and Nicole Beehum, *Teaching Adolescents to Become Learners: The Role of Noncognitive Factors in Shaping School Performance—a Critical Literature Review* (Chicago: University of Chicago Consortium on Chicago School Research, 2012).

129 **"grit"** See, for example, Angela Duckworth, *Grit: The Power of Passion* (New York: Scribner, 2016).

130 **what new employees learn** Russell Korte, "First, Get to Know Them: A Relational View of Organizational Socialization," *Human Resource Development International* 13 (2010): 27–43.

131 **performed better than acquaintance groups** Karen Jehn and Priti Shah, "Interpersonal Relationships and Task Performance: An Examination of Mediating Processes in Friendship and Acquaintance Groups," *Journal of Personality and Social Psychology* 72 (1997): 775–90.

131 **"Success travels in the company"** Steve Jamison and John Wooden, *Wooden on Leadership: A Lifetime of Observations and Reflections On and Off the Court* (New York: McGraw-Hill, 1997).

131 **connection between competence and effort** On the link between competence and success, see Herbert Simon and William Chase, "Skill in Chess," *American Scientist* 61 (1973): 394–403, who estimate that a chess master spends between ten thousand and fifty thousand hours starting at chess positions. This contention grew stronger over subsequent years: John Hayes looked at seventy-six famous classical composers and found that in almost every case, those composers did not create their greatest work until they had been composing for at least ten years; K. Anders Ericsson demonstrated the effects of "deliberate practice" in problem-solving and performance tasks; and Malcolm Gladwell popularized the "10,000 hour rule" in his book *Outliers*.

131 **bias for "naturalness"**   Chia-Jung Tsay and Mahzarin Banaji, "Naturals and Strivers: Preferences and Beliefs about Sources of Achievement," *Journal of Experimental Social Psychology* 47 (2011): 460–65.

132 **"We're likely to say"**   Tsay and Banaji, "Naturals and Strivers," 464.

133 **"job crafting"**   Amy Wrzesniewski, Justin Berg, Adam Grant, Jennifer Kurkoski, and Brian Welle, "Job-Crafting in Motion: Achieving Sustainable Gains in Happiness and Performance" (working paper, 2012).

134 **positive motivational effect**   Edward Deci and Richard Ryan, *Intrinsic Motivation and Self-Determination in Human Behavior* (New York: Plenum, 1985).

135 **"The impact of financial incentives"**   Roland Fryer, "Financial Incentives and Student Achievement: Evidence from Randomized Trials," *Quarterly Journal of Economics* 126 (2011): 1755–98. The findings of the Capital Gains program are documented by Paul Tough, *Helping Children Succeed* (New York: Houghton-Mifflin Harcourt, 2016). Fryer's quotes and statistics appear on pages 57–58.

136 **the hard work of working hard**   Or this variation: "I learned the value of hard work by working hard," attributed to Margaret Mead.

136 **"greater praise and greater honing"**   David Brooks, *The Road to Character* (New York: Random House, 2015), 255.

136 **researchers at UCLA**   Alexander W. Astin, Sarah A. Parrott, William S. Korn, and Linda J. Sax, "The American Freshman: Thirty Year Trends, 1966–1996" (Higher Education Research Institute, Graduate School of Education and Information Studies, University of California, Los Angeles, 1997).

137 **expected to become millionaires**   "Sixty-Five Per Cent of College Students Think They Will Become Millionaires," Ernst & Young survey, August 31, 2001.

137 **pioneering and popular work**   Carol Dweck, *Mindset: The New Psychology of Success* (New York: Ballantine, 2006).

138 **"Too many kids today"**   Jessica Lahey, personal interview, December 3, 2015, and March 15, 2016. All of this chapter's subsequent quotations from Lahey come from this interview unless otherwise noted.

139 **SE2R feedback model**   Mark Barnes, "SE2R Can Revolutionize How We Assess Learning," *Advanc-Ed Source*, Spring 2014, retrieved July 12, 2016, www.advanc-ed.org/source/se2r-can-revolutionize-how-we-assess-learning.

139 **"A grade is not necessarily that helpful"**   Farrington's quotes appear in Mikhail Zinshteyn, "What Does It Mean to Have Grit in the Classroom?" *Atlantic*, July 23, 2015, retrieved May 22, 2016, www.theatlantic.com/education/archive/2015/07/what-grit-looks-like-in-the-classroom/399197.

140   **persevere in the face of challenges**   Albert Bandura, *Self-Efficacy: The Exercise of Control* (New York: Freeman Press, 1997).

140   **small as a Post-it note**   David Yeager, Valerie Purdie-Vaughns, Julio Garcia, Nancy Apfel, Patti Brzustoski, Allison Master, William Hessert, Matthew Williams, and Geoffrey Cohen, "Breaking the Cycle of Mistrust: Wise Interventions to Provide Critical Feedback across the Racial Divide," *Journal of Experimental Psychology* 143 (2014): 804–24.

141   **two Wharton professors**   The survey by Ethan Mollick and Matthew Bidwell can be found at http://beacon.wharton.upenn.edu/entrepreneurship/2012/07/entrepreneurial-careers-and-happiness.

142   **no one listening along could name that tune**   Elizabeth Newton, "Overconfidence in the Communication of Intent: Heard and Unheard Melodies" (PhD diss., Stanford University, 1990).

142   **speak in concrete language**   Dan Heath and Chip Heath, "The Curse of Knowledge," *Harvard Business Review*, December 2006.

CONCLUSION

147   **"interrupt the process of forgetting"**   Peter Brown, Henry Roediger, and Mark McDaniel, *Make It Stick: The Science of Successful Learning* (Cambridge, MA: Belknap Press of Harvard University Press, 2014), 28.

About the Author

Joe Hirsch is an educator, leadership coach, and speaker. He earned an MA in education from Yeshiva University, where he directs an education startup and is completing an EdD with a concentration in instructional leadership and innovation. His work has appeared in the *Wall Street Journal, Educational Leadership*, and other leading publications. This is his first book.

CONNECT WITH THE AUTHOR

For bonus material and access to exclusive book resources, visit www.The FeedbackFix.com.

Follow the author @joemhirsch